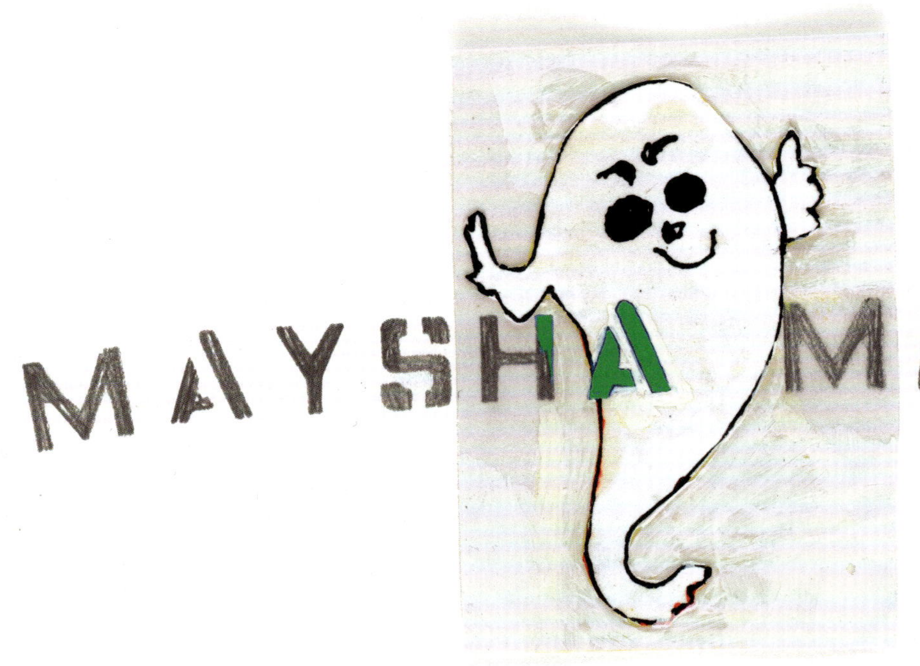

MAYSHA MOHAMEDI

MAYSHA THE FOOL

PACE GALLERY
MARCH 2026

HOT PINK:

At a Sweet Sixteen birthday party,
a heart cake with roses and lilies of the valley
seems so original.

For Mother's Day, a bouquet of mixed flowers
is very appropriate.

"Snoutitude"

3.7.25

Pale Pink:

Titanium White
Radiant Red

Darker Rose:

Warm White
A. Crimson
Dianthus Pink
Cad Yellow Med
Raw Umber

Fairy Green:

Flake White
cad yellow medium
Perm Green Light
Raw Umber

Seafoam Green:

Tit White
Warm White
Emerald Green
Perm Green Light
Cad Yellow Med
Raw Umber

White Frosting:

Tit White
Raw Umber
Dianthus Pink
Cad Yellow Medium

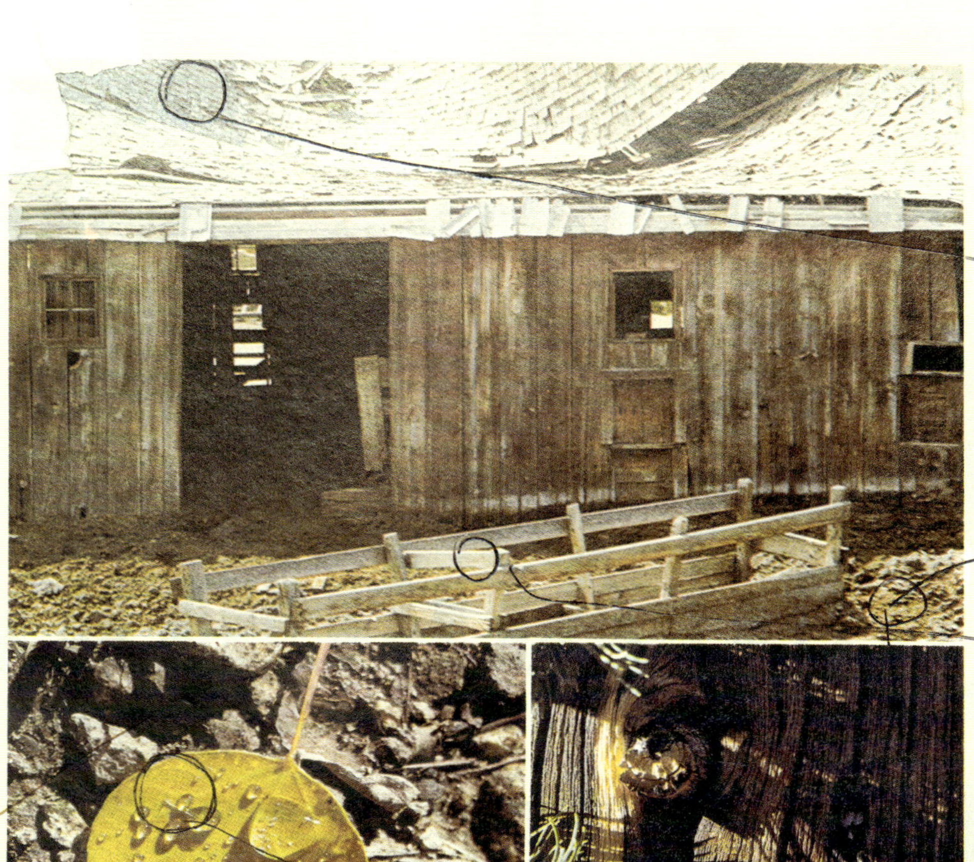

Raw Umber, A. Crimson, Cobalt Blue, Payne's Grey, Cad Lemon

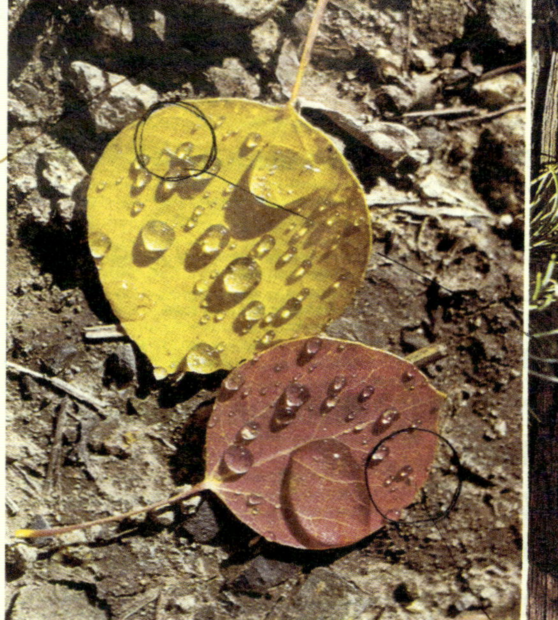

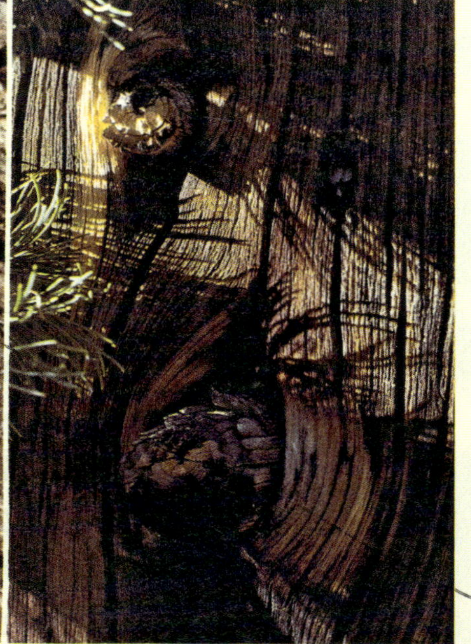

Look closely,
the season reveals
itself in small
things, too — the feel
of weather-bleached
wood, fallen leaves
in the rain, a box
of flowers drawing
warmth from the
September sun . . .

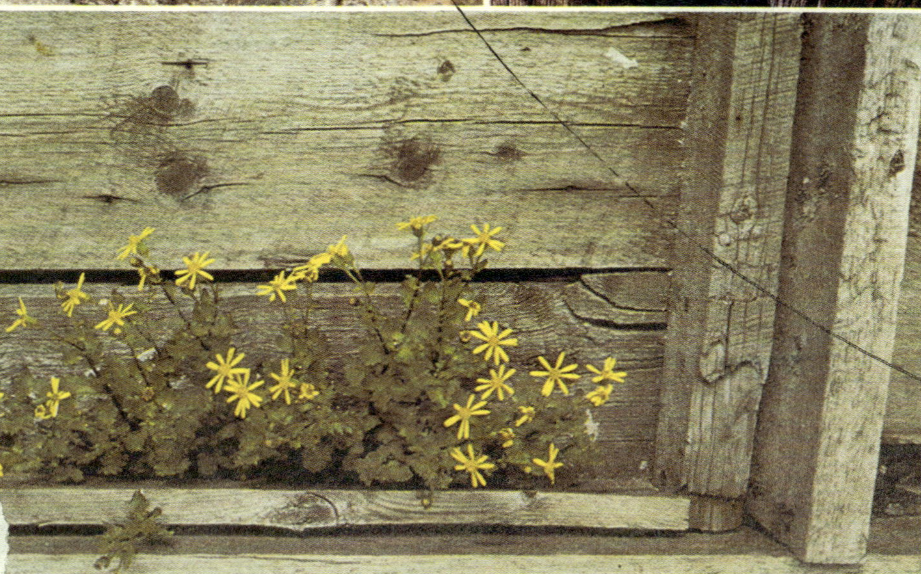

May 5, 2025

MAYSHA THE FOOL

Shadow on broken roof:

Titanium White
PG Med
Warm White
Cerulean Blue
Payne's Grey
cad yellow light
Van Dyke Brown

PIG TROUGH:

Titanium white
P G Med
Raw Sienna
Van Dyke Brown

Golden Dirt

Titanium white
Raw Sienna
Bismuth yellow
Van Dyke Brown

~~Yellow leaf~~

Warm White
Bismuth Yellow
Raw Sienna
Van Dyke Brown
cad orange

Tit White

Dusty Red Leaf

P. Grey, cad Red Med, A. crimson, Van Dyke Brown

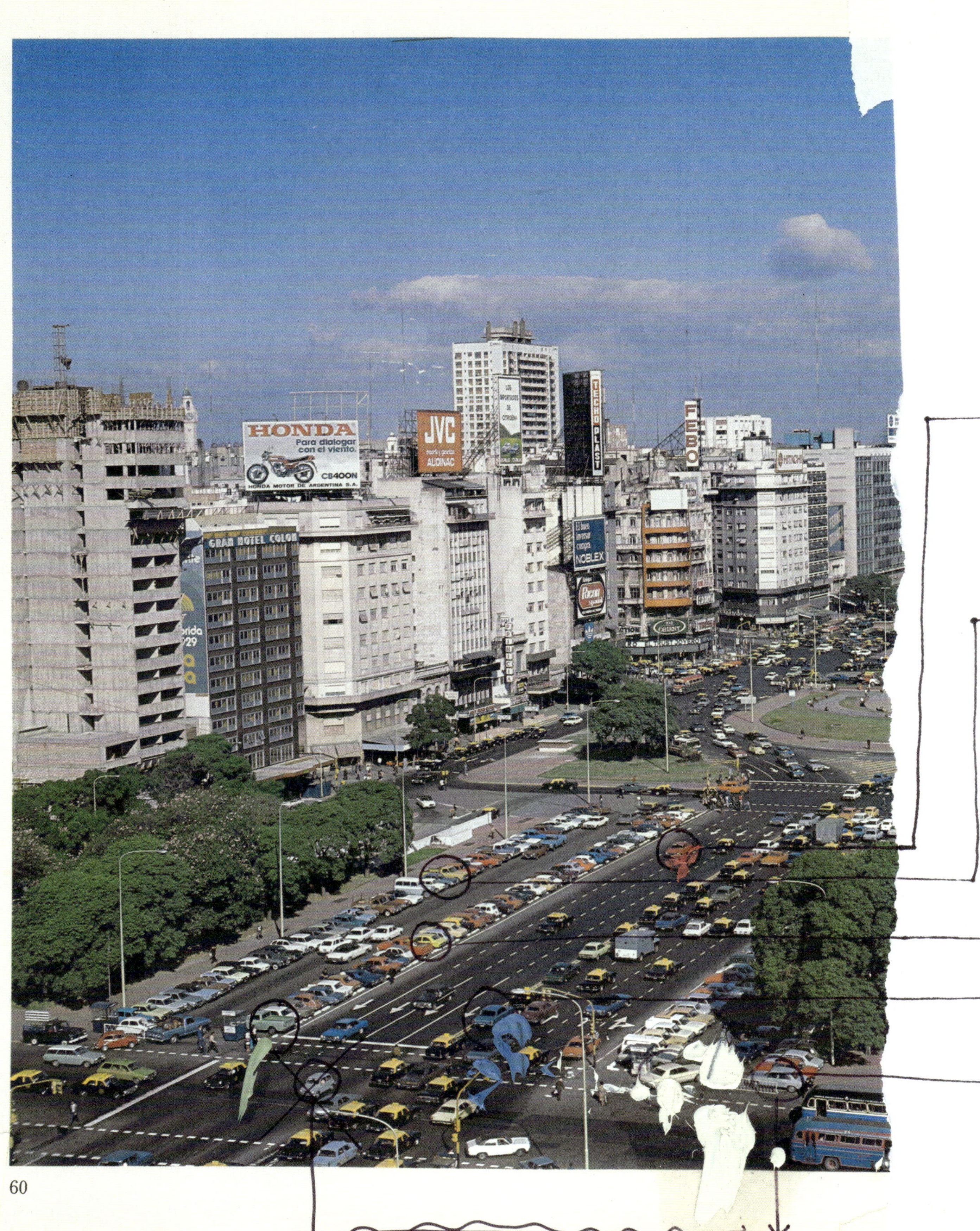

January 01, 2026

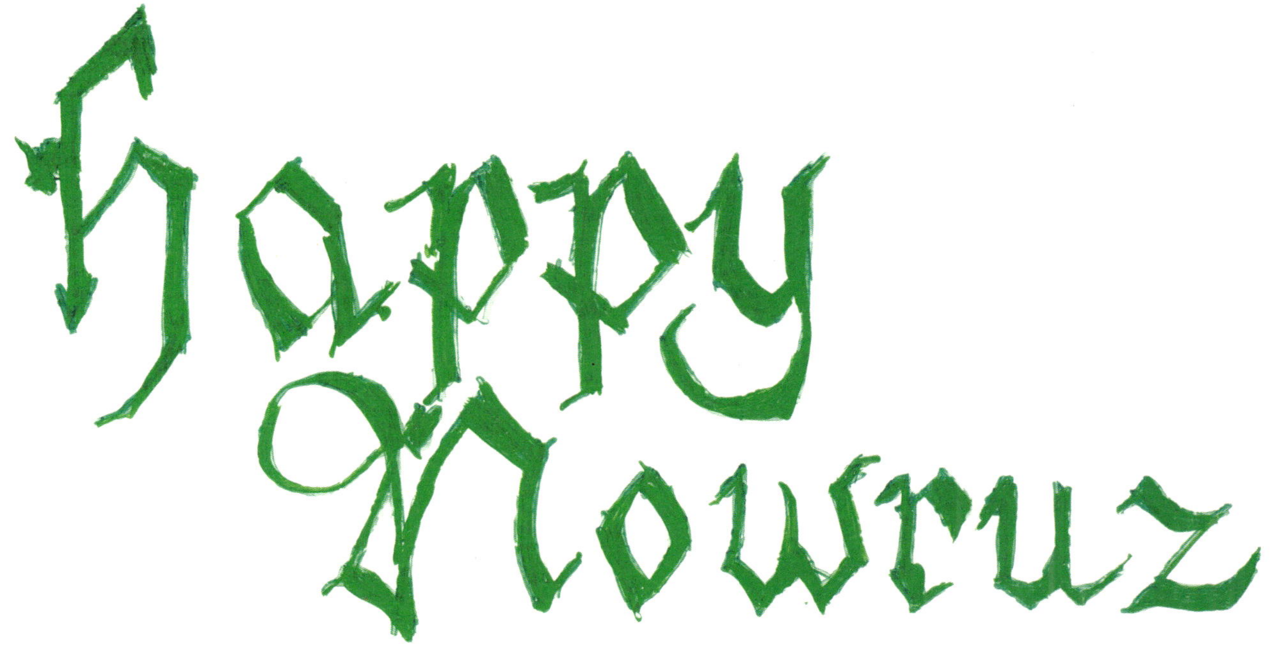

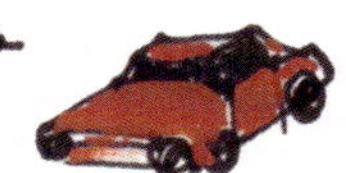

CADMIUM RED MEDIUM
WARM WHITE
RAW SIENNA

TITANIUM WHITE
ALIZARIN CRIMSON
RAW UMBER

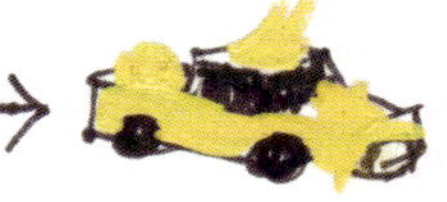

TITANIUM WHITE
BISMUTH YELLOW
NAPLES YELLOW

HANSA YELLOW MEDIUM
CADMIUM RED MEDIUM
VAN DYKE BROWN

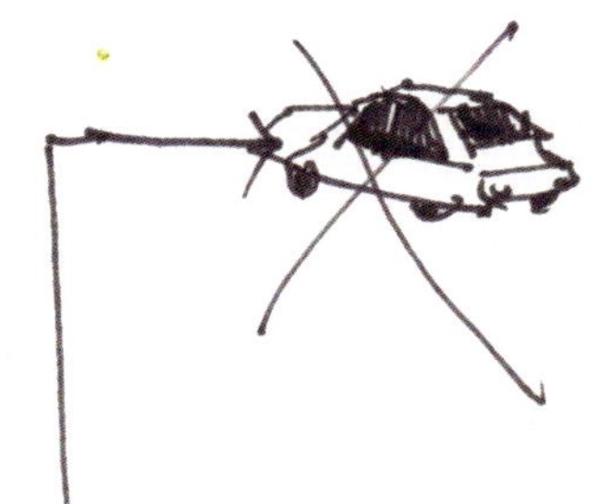

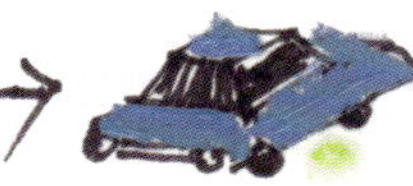

TITANIUM WHITE
CERULEAN BLUE
COBALT BLUE
PORTLAND GREY LIGHT
PORTLAND GREY DEEP

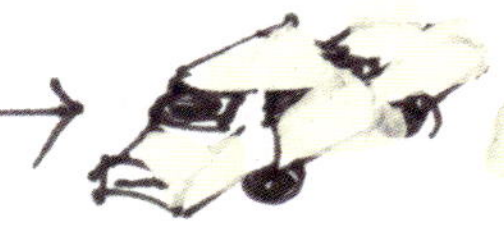

TITANIUM WHITE
BISMUTH YELLOW
PORTLAND GREY LIGHT

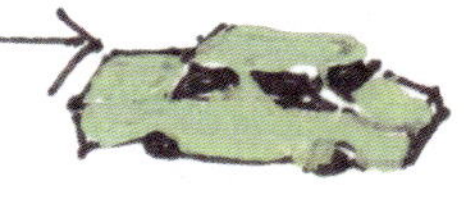

PERM GREEN LIGHT
TITANIUM WHITE
OH WARM GREY LIGHT
PAYNE'S GREY

Build-Your-Own Sundae

Here's the master plan: You supply the ingredients (your favorites from our list) and let your guests build themselves a towering sundae. For the younger kids, limit the number of ingredient choices. (Perhaps choose only two of the options in each category.) And plan on using about ½ cup of ice cream and ⅓ cup of fruit for each sundae. But for the older kids, you may need to double or even triple the choices and amounts!

- Prepare Choco-Mallow Sauce and Blueberry Sauce. Cover and chill until party time.
- Place scoops of each kind of ice cream into individual large, chilled serving bowls. Cover and freeze till serving time.
- Put sauces and sprinkles in individual containers. Cover till serving time. Chill sauces till party time.
- At party time, set out sauces, sprinkles, and sundae dishes.

Peel, remove pits, and slice nectarines. Peel and slice bananas. Dip nectarine and banana slices into *lemon juice* to prevent browning. If necessary, slice any large whole strawberries. Put fruit in individual containers. Cover till serving time.

- At serving time, remove covers from containers of ingredients. Set out ice cream. Let guests make their own sundaes by first placing some sauce in a dish, then ice cream and fruit. Top with more sauce and some sprinkles.

Sauces

Choco-Mallow Sauce *(see recipe at right)*

Blueberry Sauce *(see recipe at right)*

Caramel topping

Honey

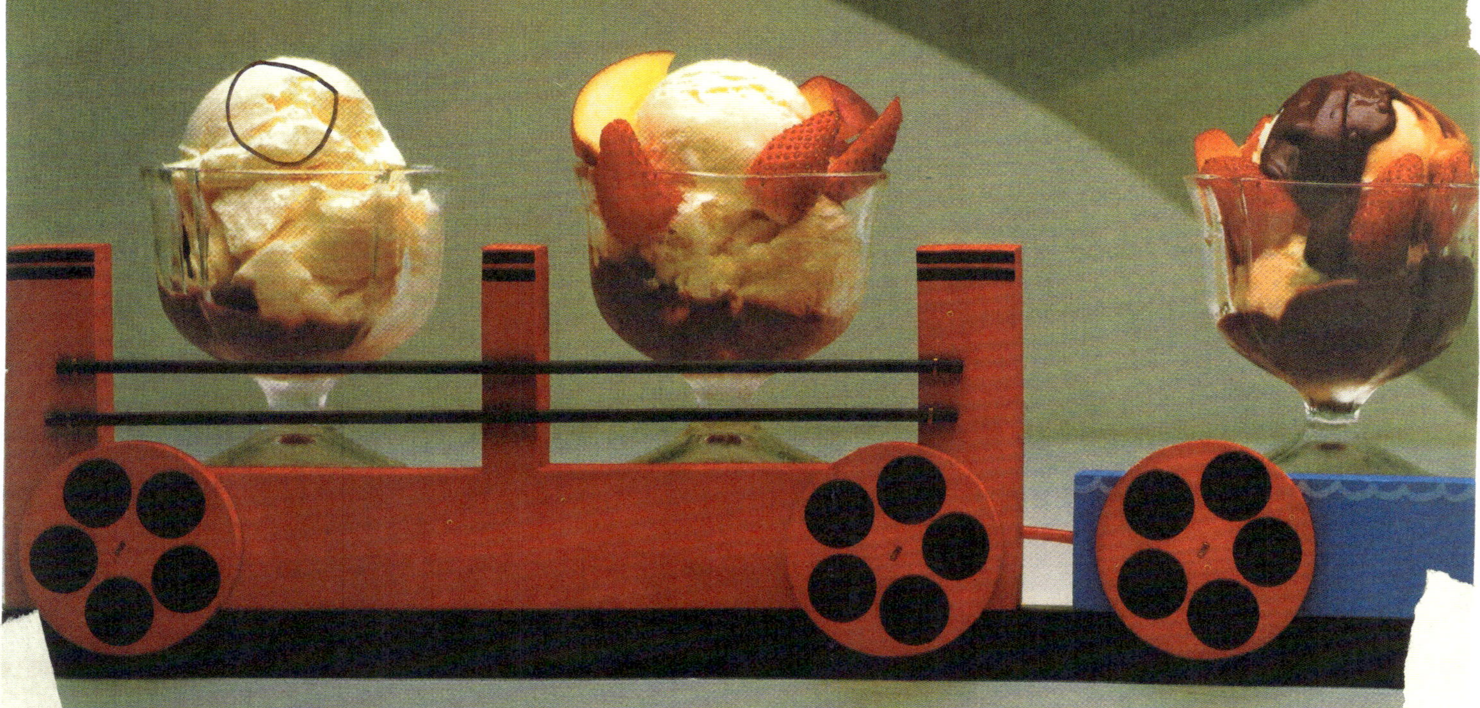

+ Ice Cream	+ Fruit	+ Sprinkles
Vanilla *or* butter pecan ice cream	Nectarines *or* canned peach slices, drained	Granola
Strawberry ice cream	Bananas	Chopped peanuts *or* sunflower nuts
Chocolate ice cream	Fresh strawberries *or* frozen unsweetened whole strawberries, thawed	Toasted coconut
	Canned pineapple tidbits, drained	Mixed dried fruit bits
		Miniature semisweet chocolate pieces

Choco-Mallow Sauce: In a small heavy saucepan melt 1½ cups *tiny marshmallows* in ¾ cup *milk* over medium heat. After marshmallows are melted, add one 6-ounce package (1 cup) *semisweet chocolate pieces*. Continue heating and stirring with a wire whisk till chocolate is melted. Remove from heat and cool slightly. Pour mixture into a serving dish. Cover and chill. At party time, set sauce out to bring to room temperature. Makes 2 cups.

Blueberry Sauce: In a small saucepan combine 2 cups fresh *or* frozen *blueberries*, 3 tablespoons *orange juice*, and 2 tablespoons *sugar*. Cook and stir over medium heat till mixture is bubbly. Remove from heat and coarsely crush the blueberries. Cool slightly. Pour mixture into a serving dish. Cover and chill. At party time, set sauce out to bring to room temperature. Makes 1½ cups.

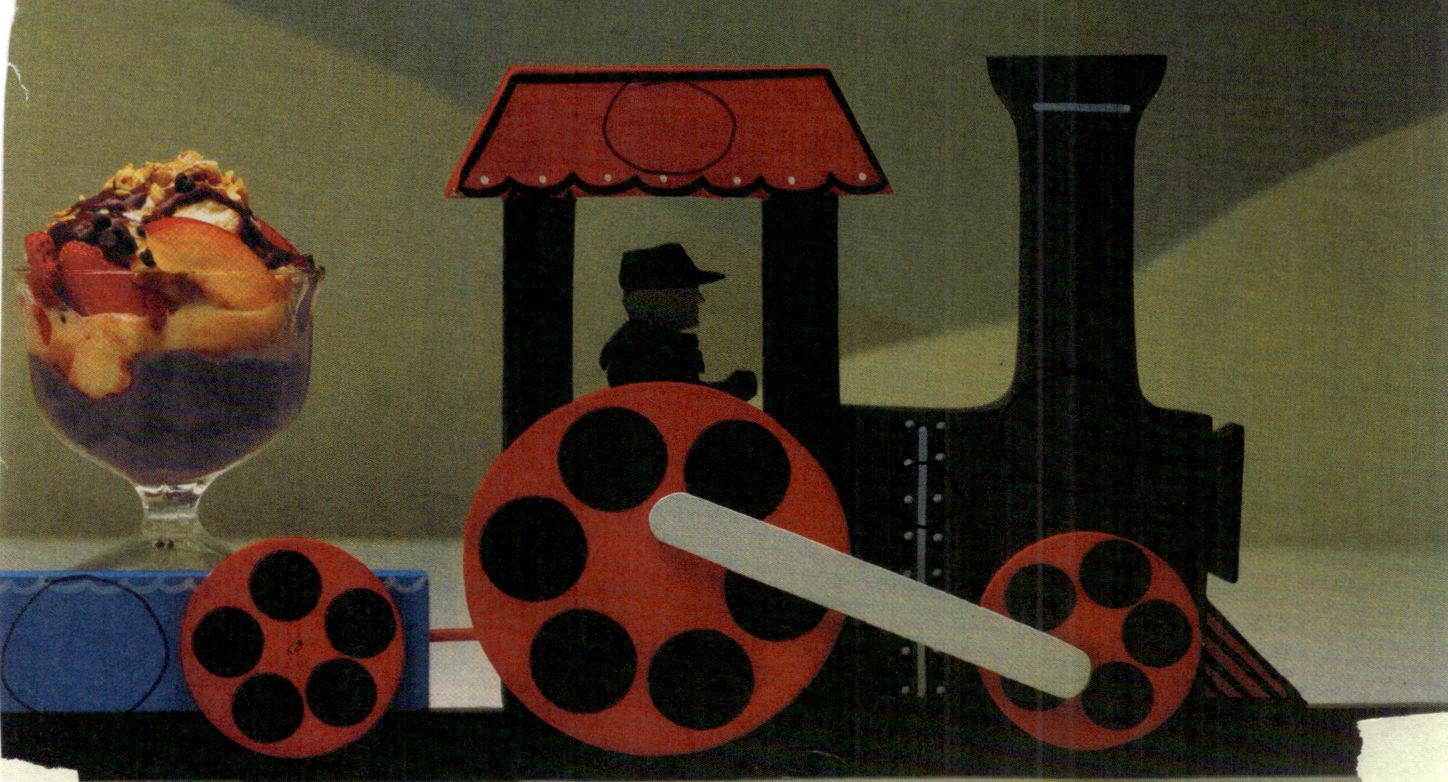

Absolute Zero 5/24/25

Green backdrop:

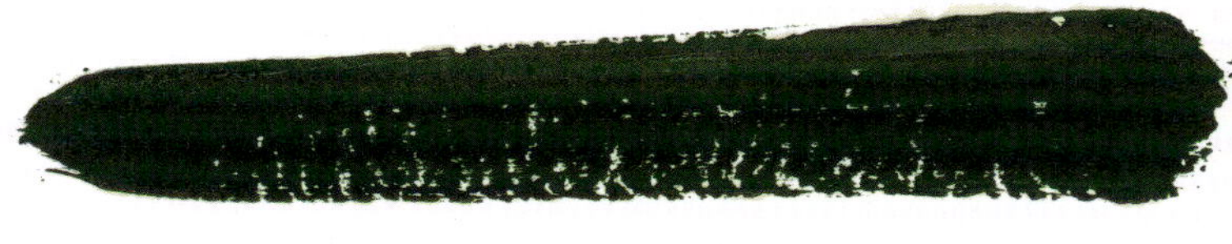

Emerald Green
Phthalo Green
Van Dyke Brown
Raw Sienna

Blue (train):

Cobalt Blue
Payne's Grey
Titanium White

Red (train):

Cad Red Medium
Alizarin Crimson
Van Dyke Brown
Flake White

Vanilla Ice Cream:

Warm White
Neutral Grey

Black (train):

check black from Tokyo show

Raw Umber
Phthalo Blue
A Crimson
PG Light

Maybe light pink from dots on train

Pastel Turquoise (train):

Phthalo Blue
Payne's Grey
Cerulean Blue
Cobalt Blue
Titanium White
Cad Yellow Light

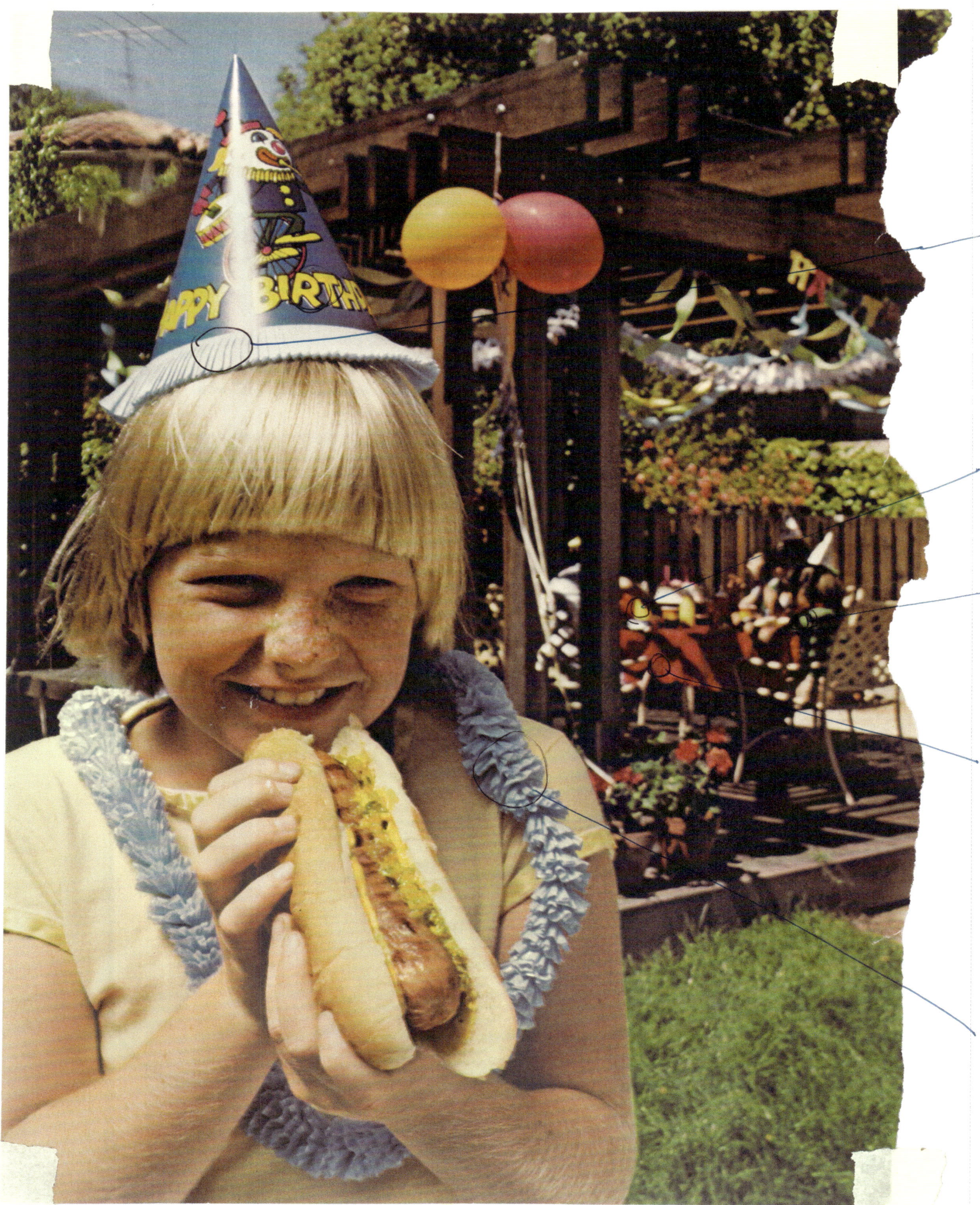

JULY 20, 2025

Saddozay

LIGHT BLUE RUFFLE:

√ Titanium White
Pthalo Blue
Raw Sienna
Van Dyke Brown

YELLOW THING:

√ Titanium White
Warm White
Cad Lemon
Cad Yellow Med

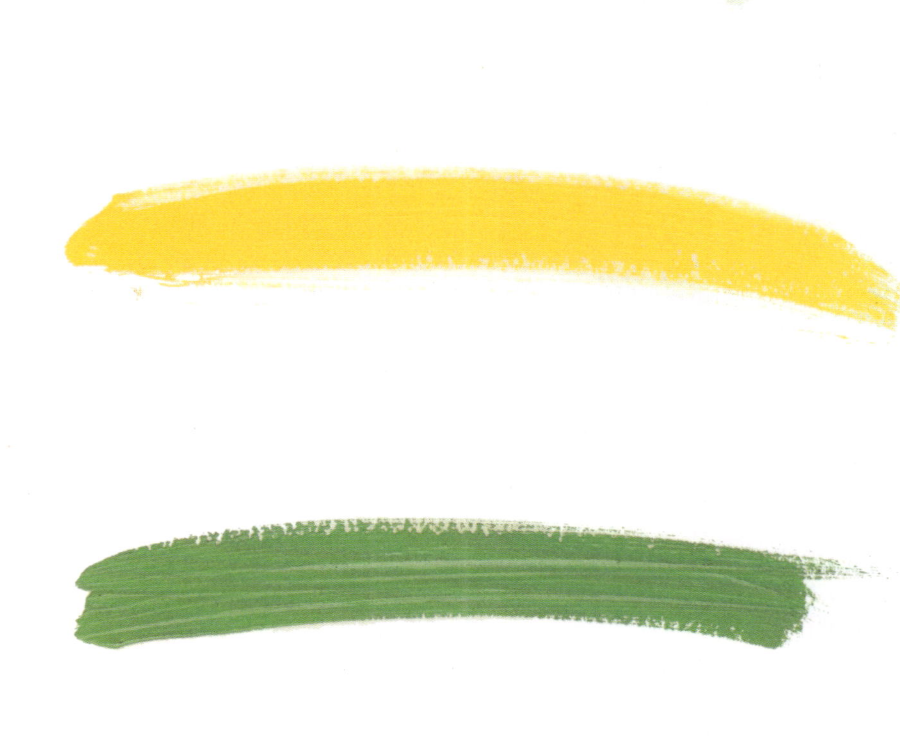

GREEN T-SHIRT:

√ Titanium White
Warm White
Emerald Green
Cad Yellow Med
Van Dyke Brown
Raw Sienna

RED TABLE CLOTH:

Cad Red Med
Cad Red Light
Portlan Warm Grey
Van Dyke Brown
√ Titanium White
Alizarin Crimson

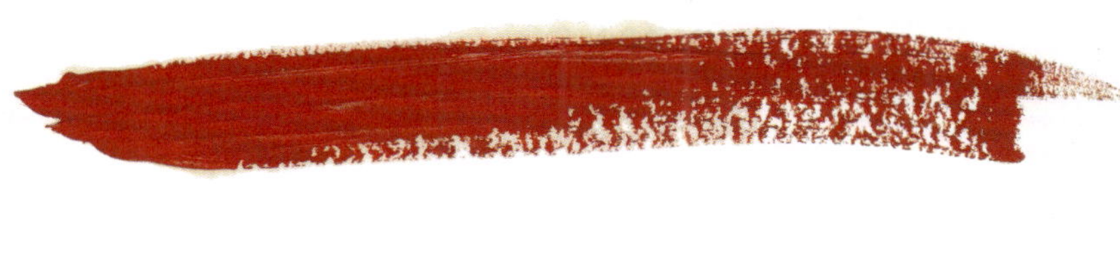

BLUE LEI:

Portland Warm Grey
Cobalt Blue
Pthalo Blue
Flake White
Radiant Violet

Hooker's Green
Emerald Green
Cad yellow light
PG light
Van Dyke Brown
Raw Umber

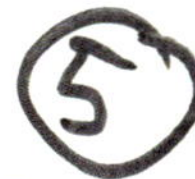

12

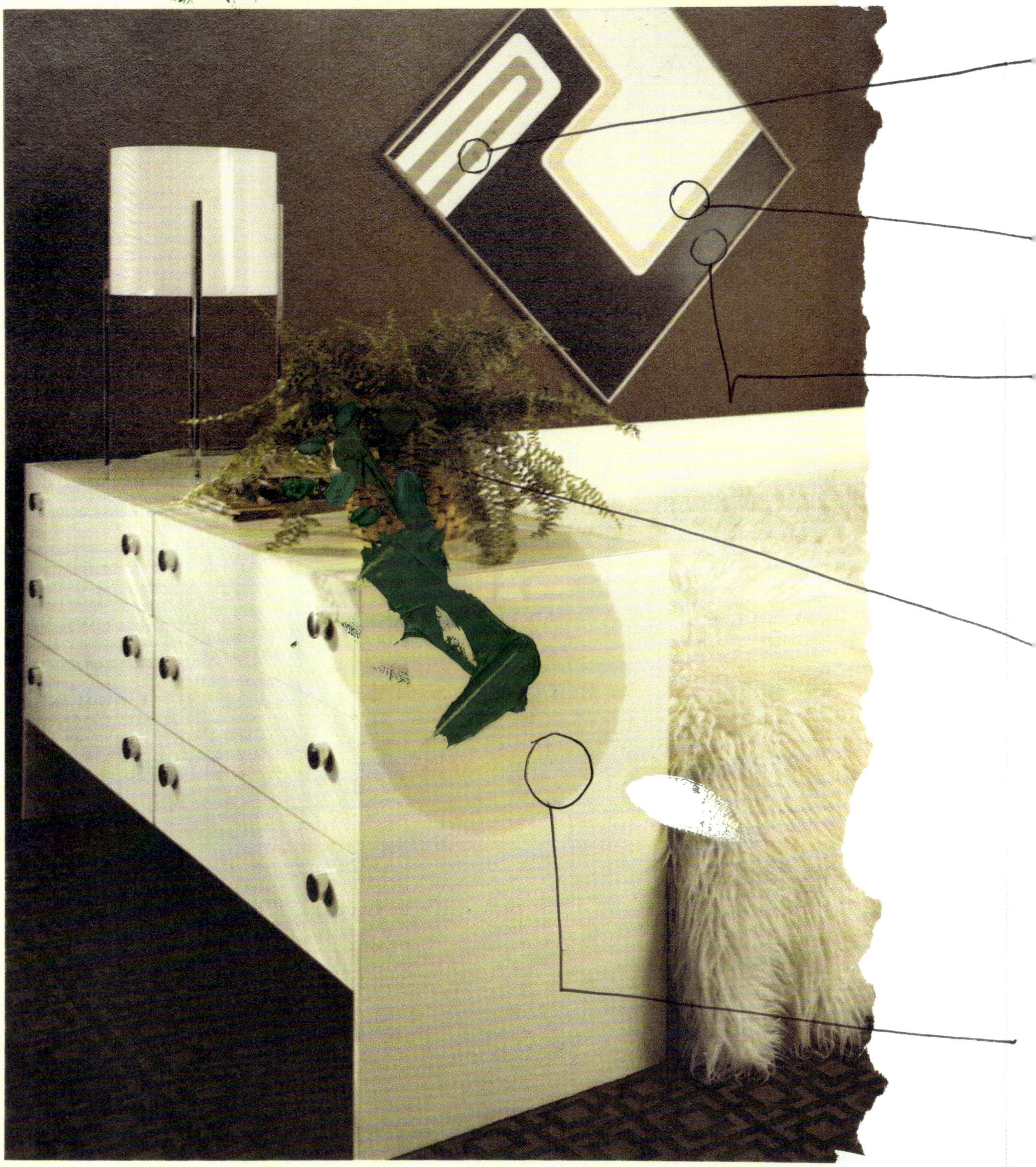

RATS!

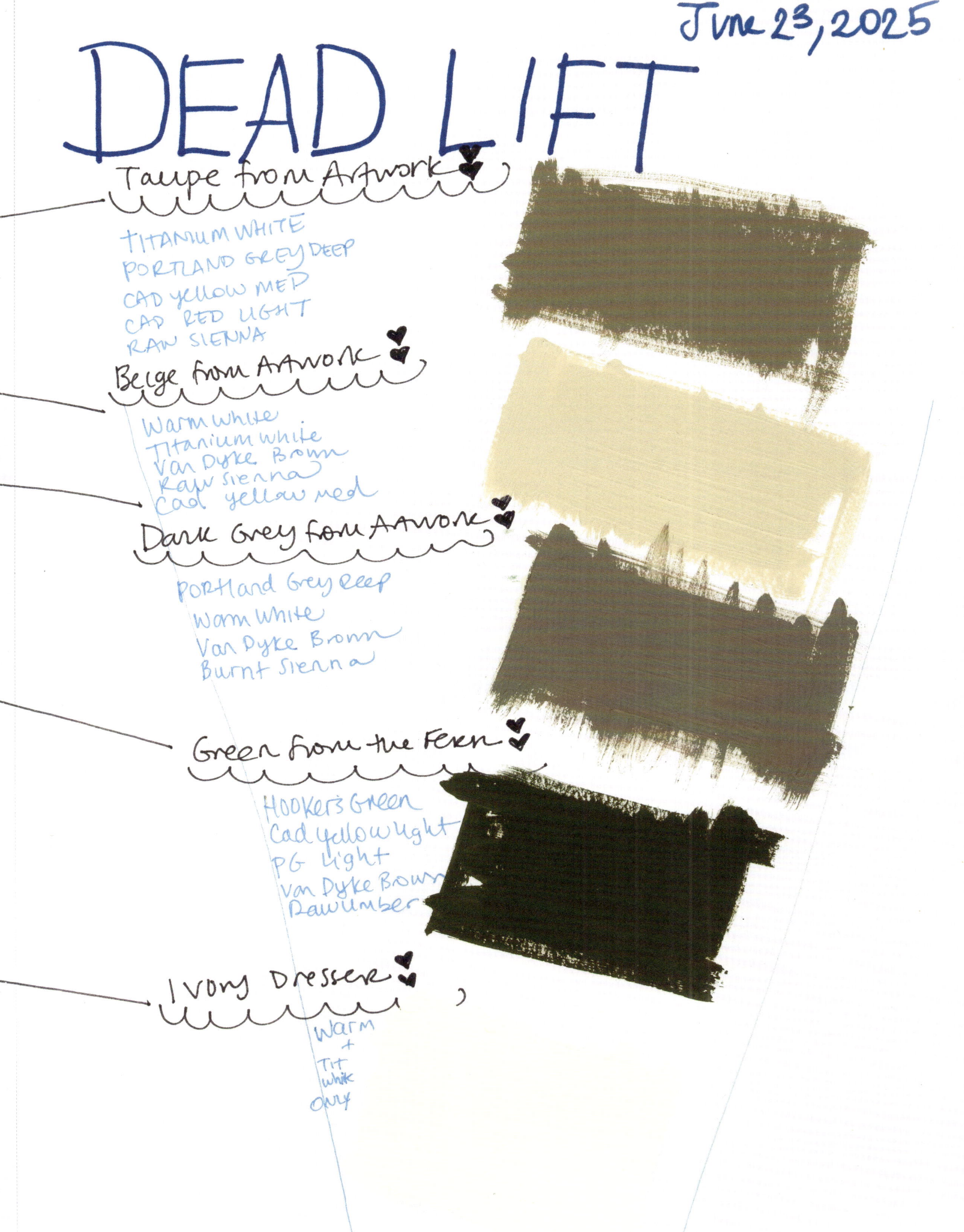
June 23, 2025
DEAD LIFT
Taupe from Artwork
TITANIUM WHITE
PORTLAND GREY DEEP
CAD YELLOW MED
CAD RED LIGHT
RAW SIENNA
Beige from Artwork
Warm white
Titanium white
Van Dyke Brown
Raw Sienna
Cad yellow med
Dark Grey from Artwork
Portland Grey Deep
Warm White
Van Dyke Brown
Burnt Sienna
Green from the Fern
Hooker's Green
Cad yellow light
PG light
Van Dyke Brown
Raw Umber
Ivory Dresser
Warm
+
Tit
white
ONLY

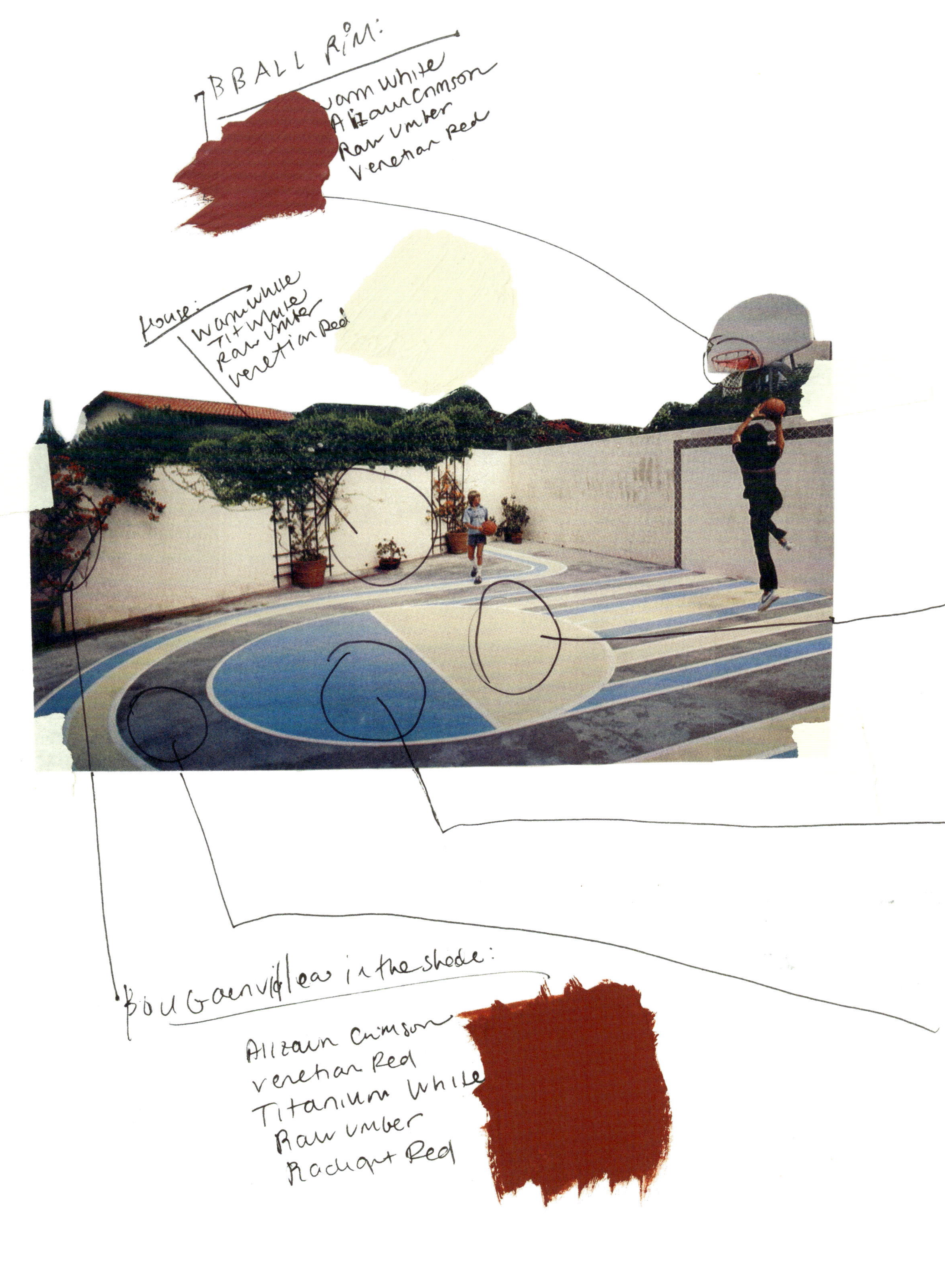

BBALL RIM:
Warm White
Alizarin Crimson
Raw Umber
Venetian Red
House:
Warm White
Ti+White
Raw Umber
Venetian Red
Bougainvillea in the shade:
Alizarin Crimson
Venetian Red
Titanium White
Raw Umber
Radiant Red

Feb. 1, 2025

SKY LEILA

EGGSHELL-TOP:

titanium white
warm white
raw umber
raw sienna

BLUE-TOP:

portland Gray Light
pthalo Blue
cobalt blue
A. crimson

Black TOP:

Payne's gray
P G Medium
tit white

JANUARY 01. 2025

The QABALISTIC TAROT

A TEXTBOOK OF MYSTICAL PHILOSOPHY

Robert Wang

LIGHT YELLOW

I DON'T MIND WHAT HAPPENS.

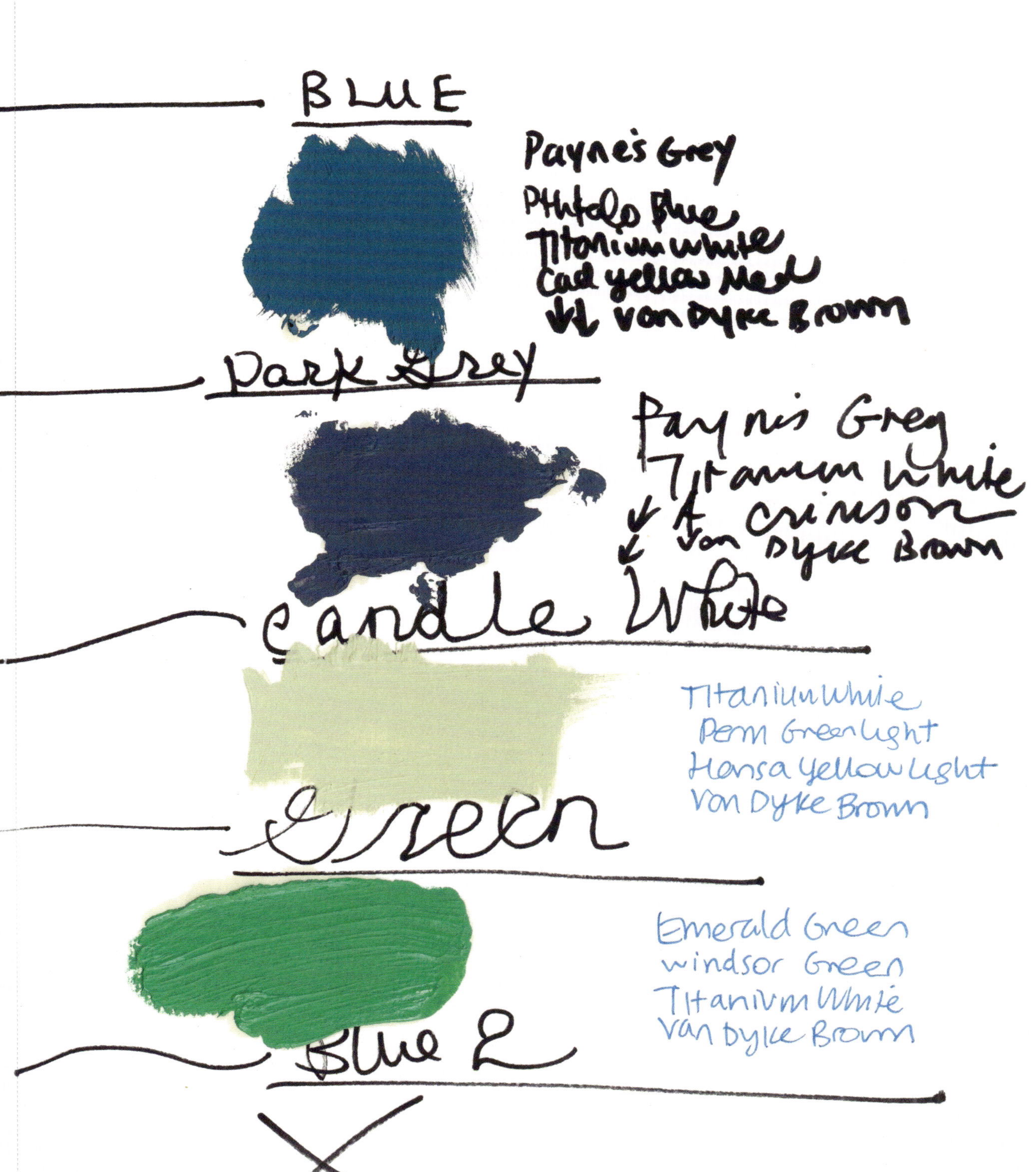

= Cad yellow light
cad yellow med
Tit white
Raw umber

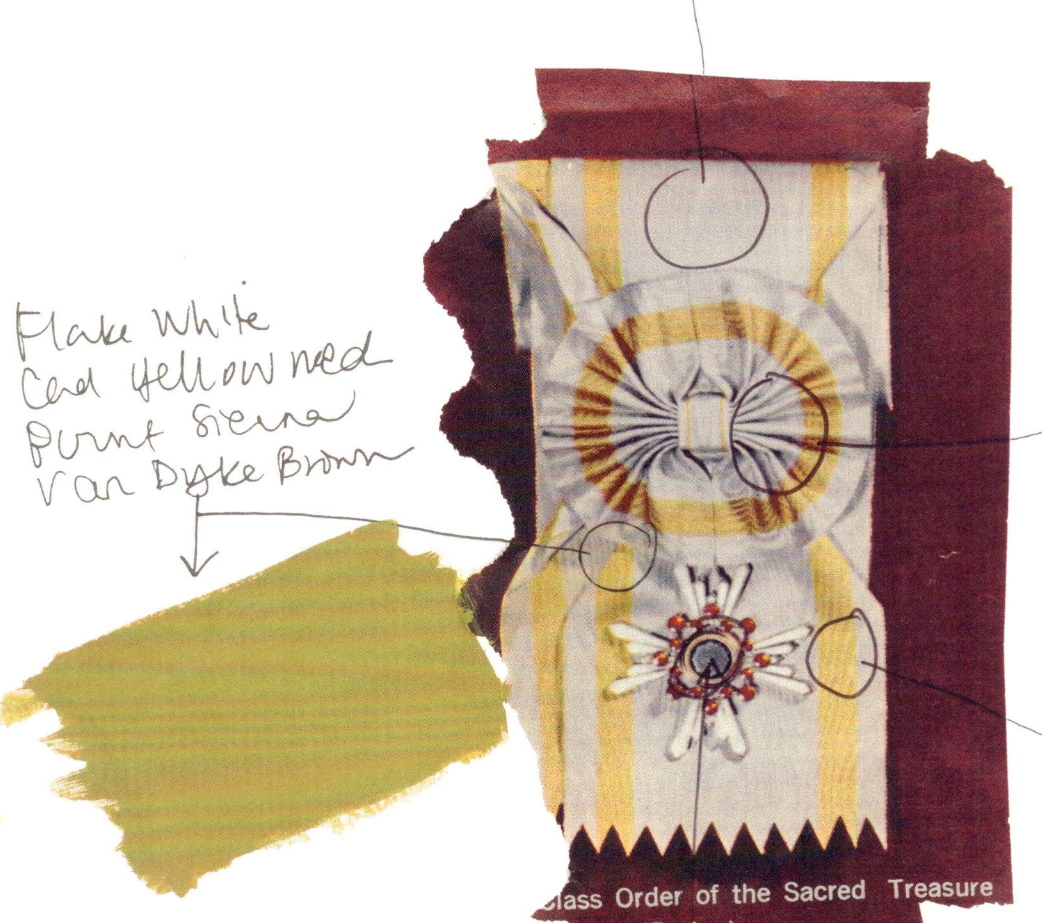

April 13, 2025

17 x 15 inches.

Wit

for Suzanne's class
Acting 1

Light Grey

Flake White Replacement
Portland Grey Light
Payne's Grey
A. Crimson

Light Lavender

PG Light
Flake White
Payne's Grey
A. Crimson

Ribbon Yellow

Warm White
Cad Yellow Med
Raw Sienna

Periwinkle

Portland Grey Deep
Flake White
Cobalt Blue
A Crimson
Payne's Grey

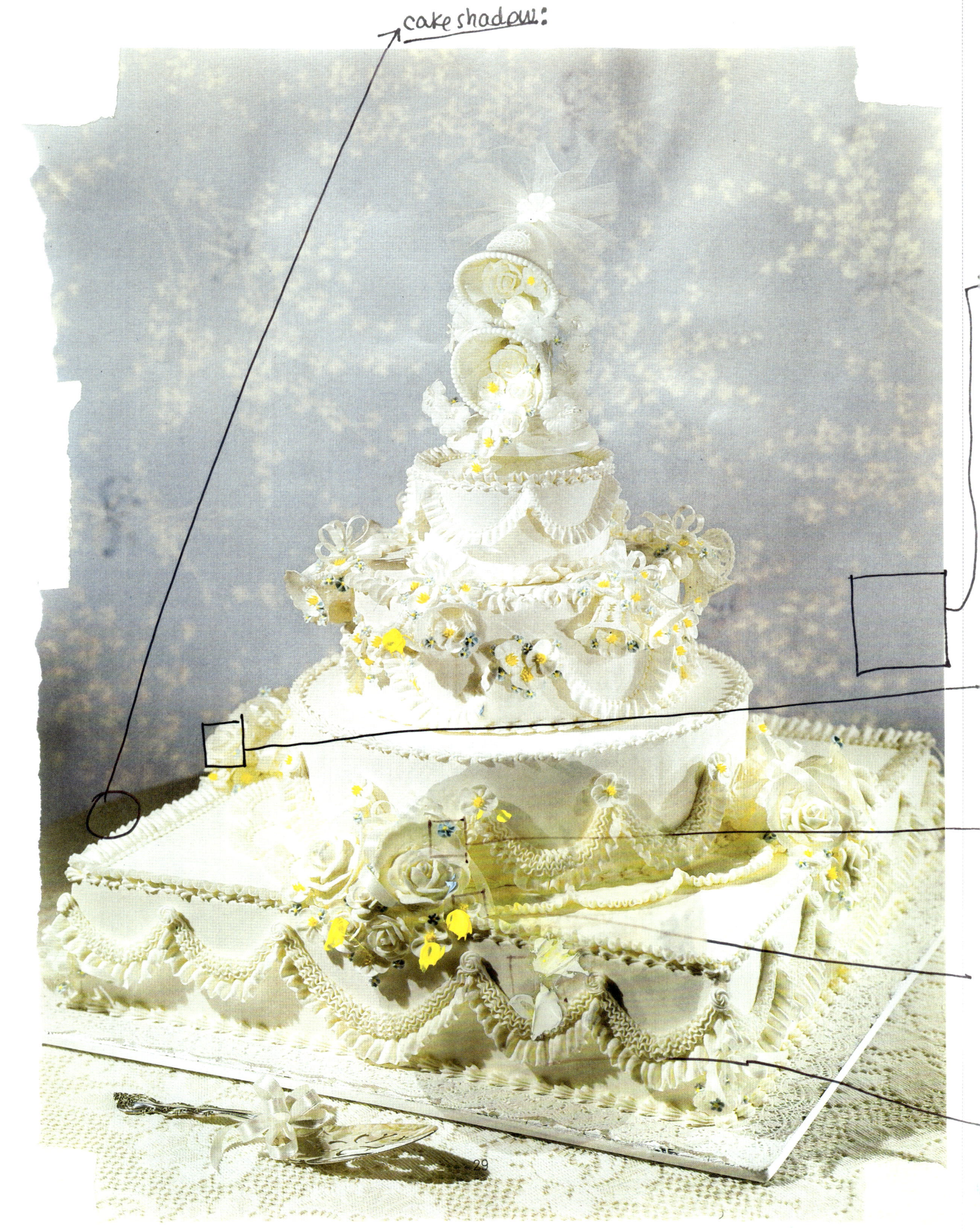
cake shadow:

O Thy Living God;
Unlock These Hands;
Unlock this Heart;
Amen

9/9/25

→ Lavender:

TITANIUM WHITE
DH Kings Blue Deep
P. W. Grey

→ satiny soft yellow white:

TITANIUM White
↓ Warm White
↓ Bismuth Vanadate yellow
↓ PG Light

~~Blue Petals~~ Frosting Shadow:

PG Light
Titanium white
PG Medium
Bismuth Vanadate yellow

→ yellow petals:

Cadmium yellow medium
Hansa yellow medium
Titanium White

→ ~~Frosting Shadow~~: Blue Petals:

Titanium White
Cerulean Blue

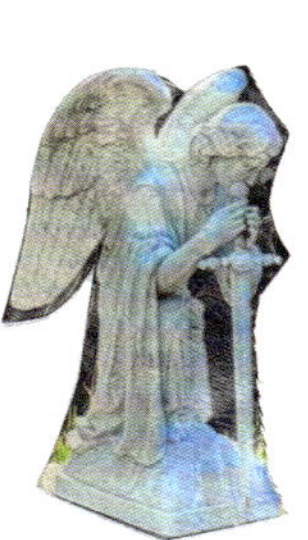
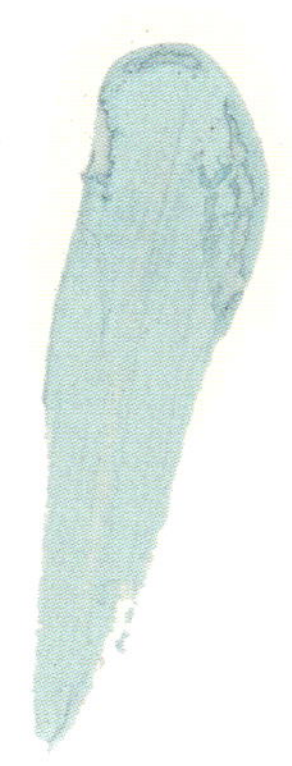
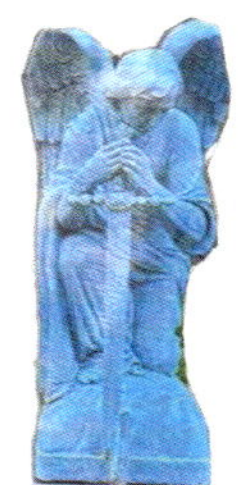
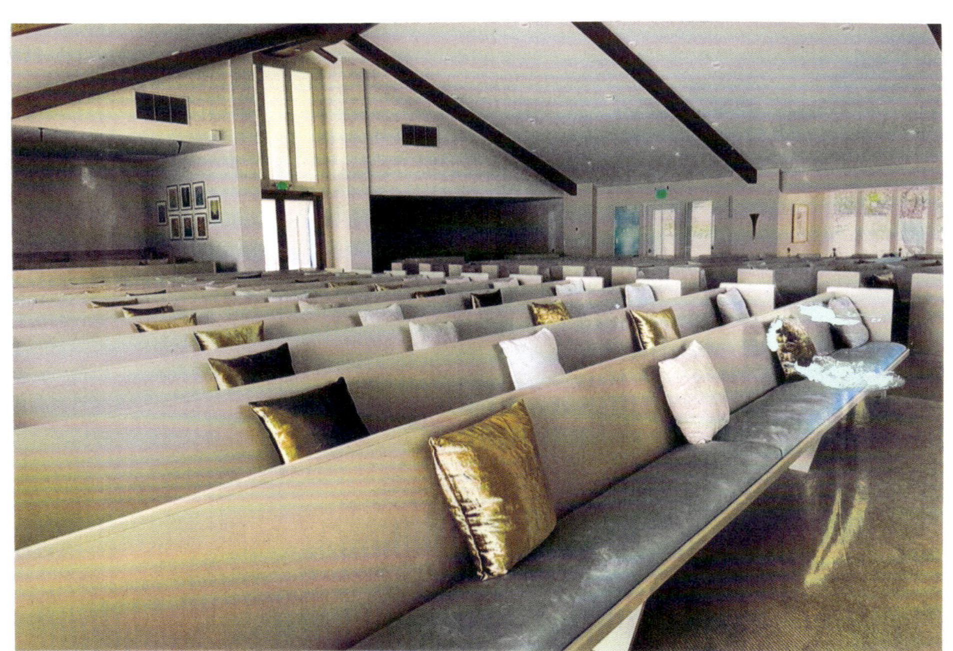
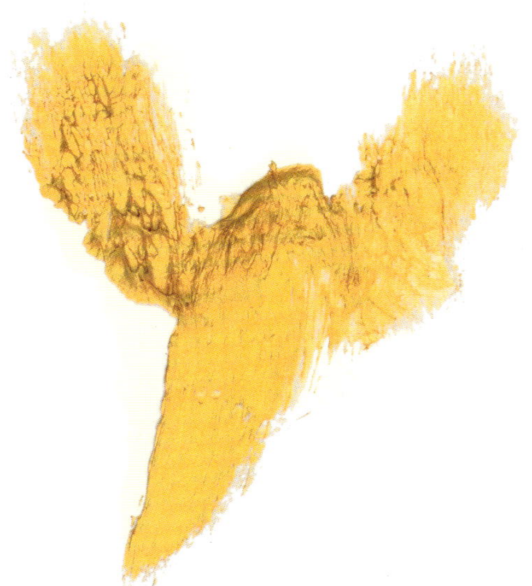

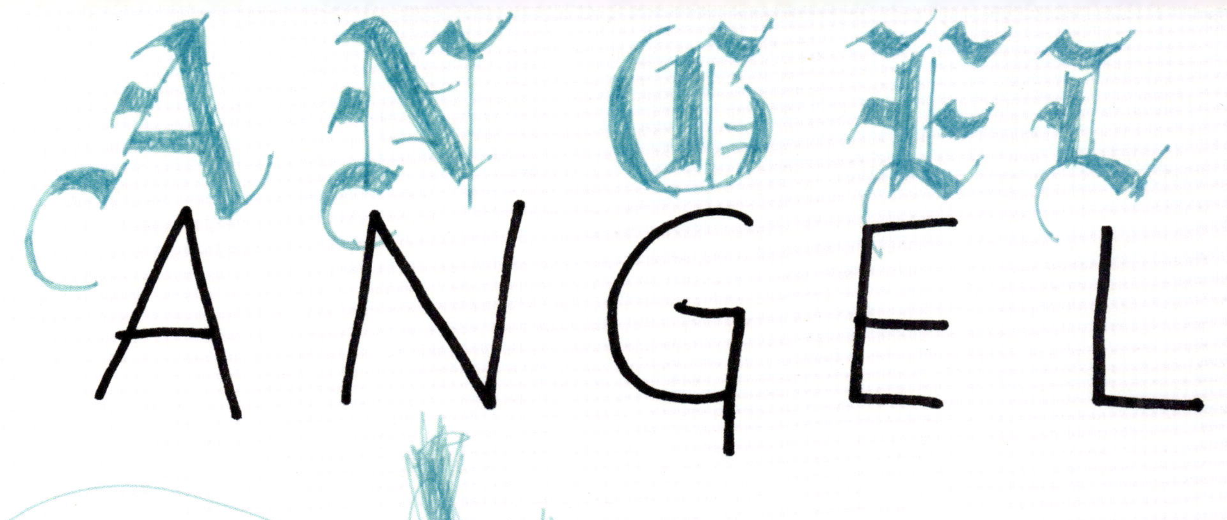

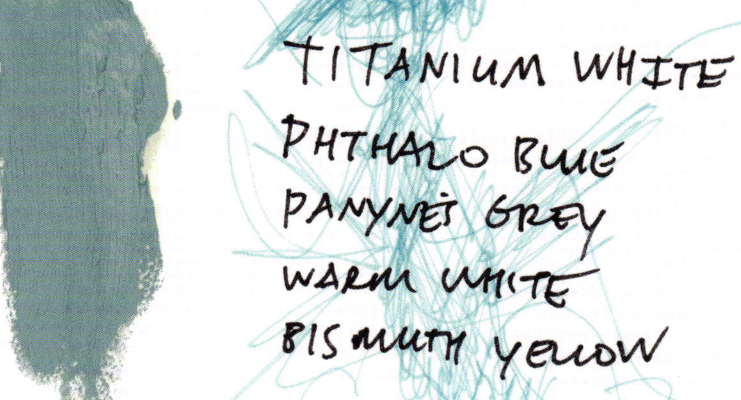

TITANIUM WHITE
PHTHALO BLUE
PANYNES GREY
WARM WHITE
BISMUTH YELLOW

WARM WHITE
CAD YELLOW LIGHT
Raw Sienna
VAN DYKE BROWN

WARM WHITE
P.G. LIGHT.

side track on outdoor fun. Your MG dealer will arrange it.

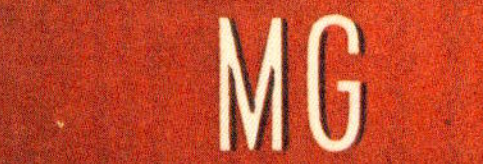

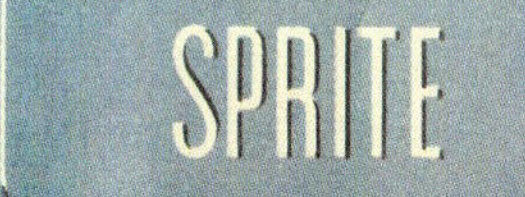

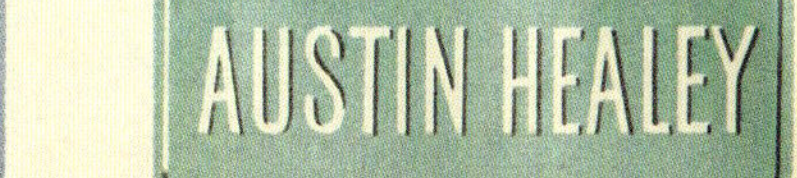

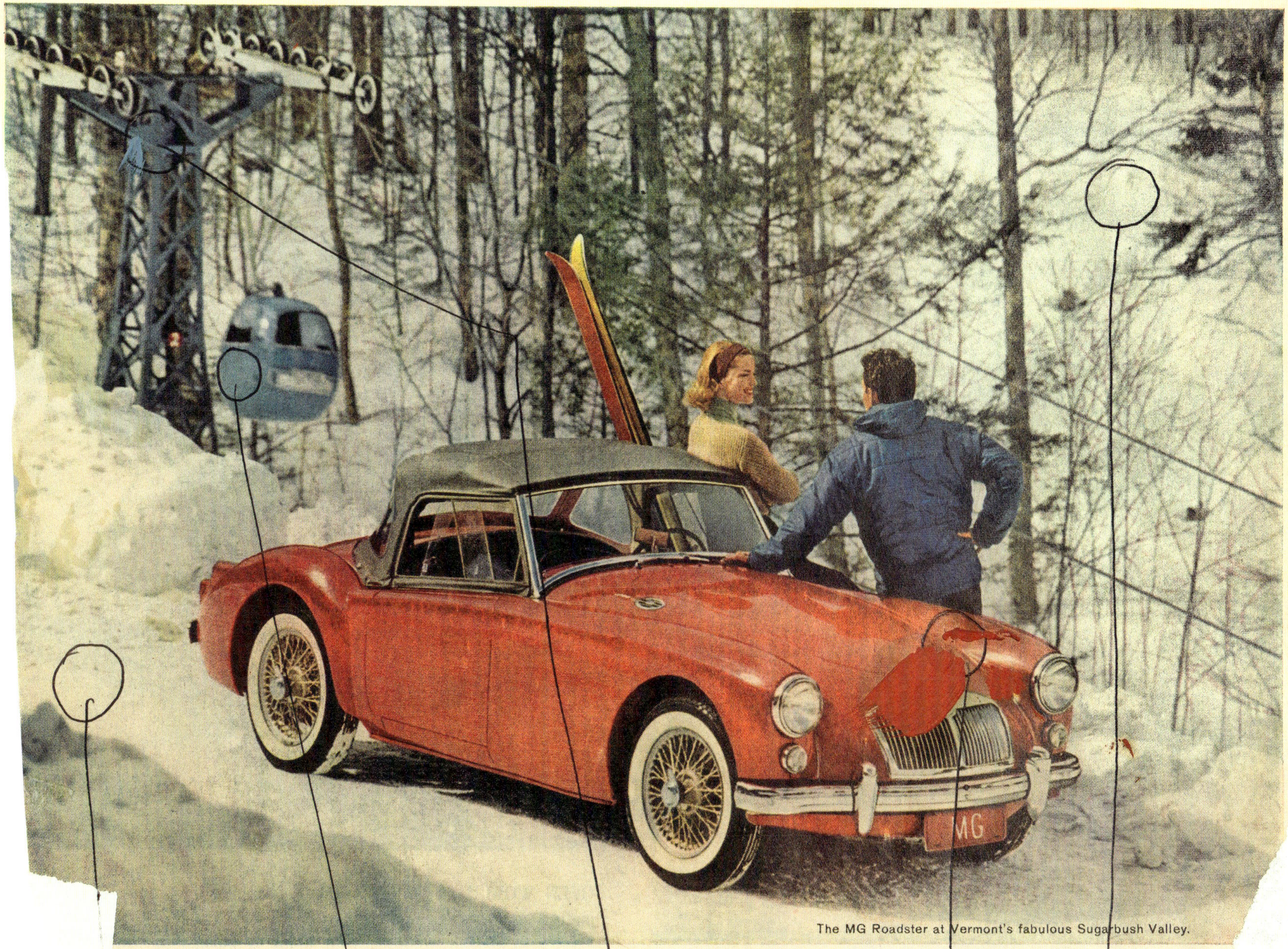

The MG Roadster at Vermont's fabulous Sugarbush Valley.

Going abroad? Have a BMC car meet you on arrival. Write for

AUDITION 8/8/25

Darker snow on Hillside:

Warm White
Portland Grey Light
Payne's Grey
Raw Umber

Cad yellow med
Van Dyke Brown

Roadster Red:

Cad Red Med
Warm White
A. crimson
Cad yellow med
Raw Umber

+ Burnt Sienna
+ PG Deep
+ ~~Raw~~ Sienna

Ski Lift Tower Blue (Darker ~~Lighter~~):

Flake White
Cerulean Blue
Payne's Grey
Cobalt Blue

Cad yellow med
Raw Umber

+ INDANTHRONE BLUE
↓ PG Deep

Ski Lift Pod Blue (Lighter):

Flake White
Cerulean Blue
Payne's Grey
Cobalt Blue

Raw Umber
Cad Yellow Med

Lighter snow in foreground:

Flake White
Cad yellow med
Payne's Grey
Raw Umber

he Shaker table setting above. A pair of folk figures, with
ppliquéd to the Belgian linen and polyester cloth to decorate
cherries is repeated on the napkins. Reproductions of Shaker boxes
cinnamon sticks. The Midwest farmhouse setting below has a Biblical theme.
farm animals is shaped from baker's clay and baked in the oven. A variety of
and white cotton prints were sewn together patchwork-style to make the tablecloth. Blue
were trimmed with matching prints. All the designs and styling are by Joanne Beretta.

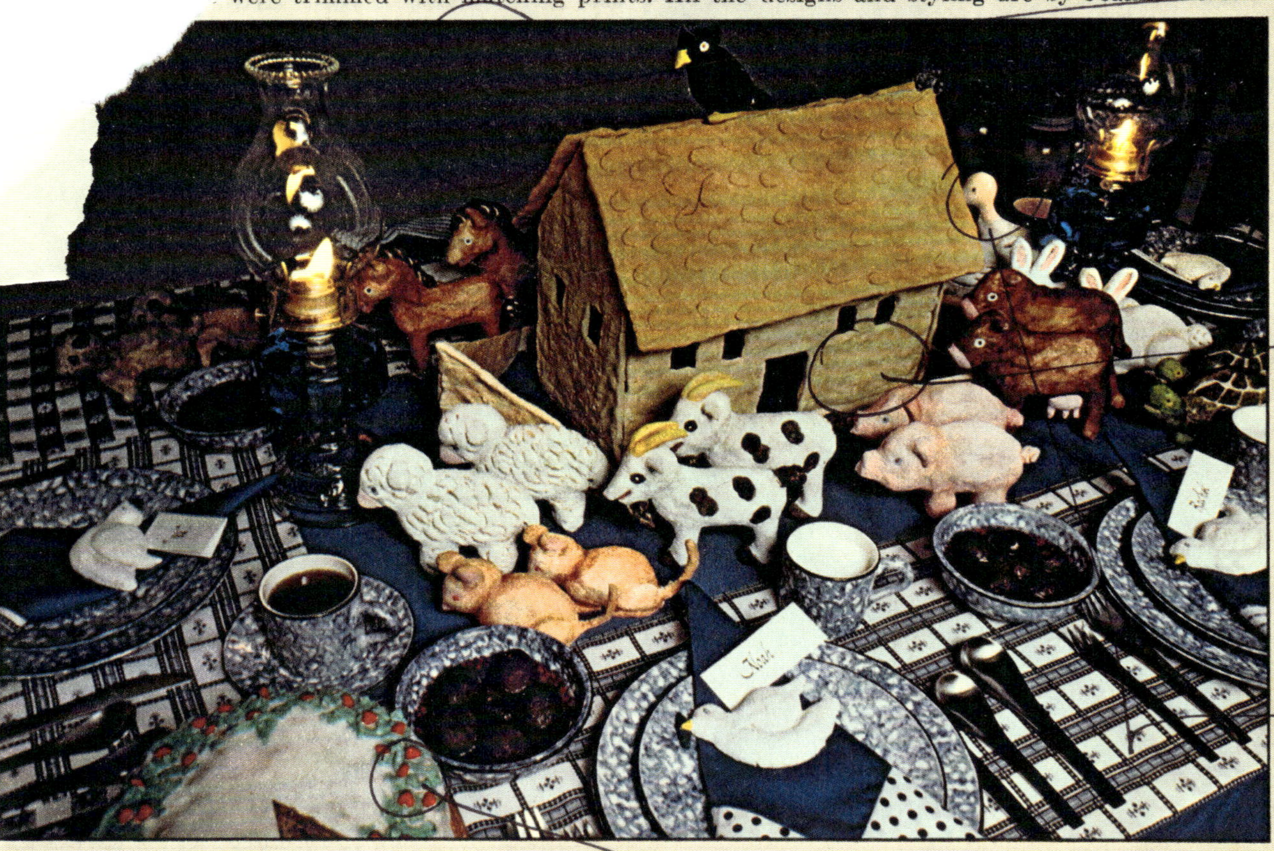

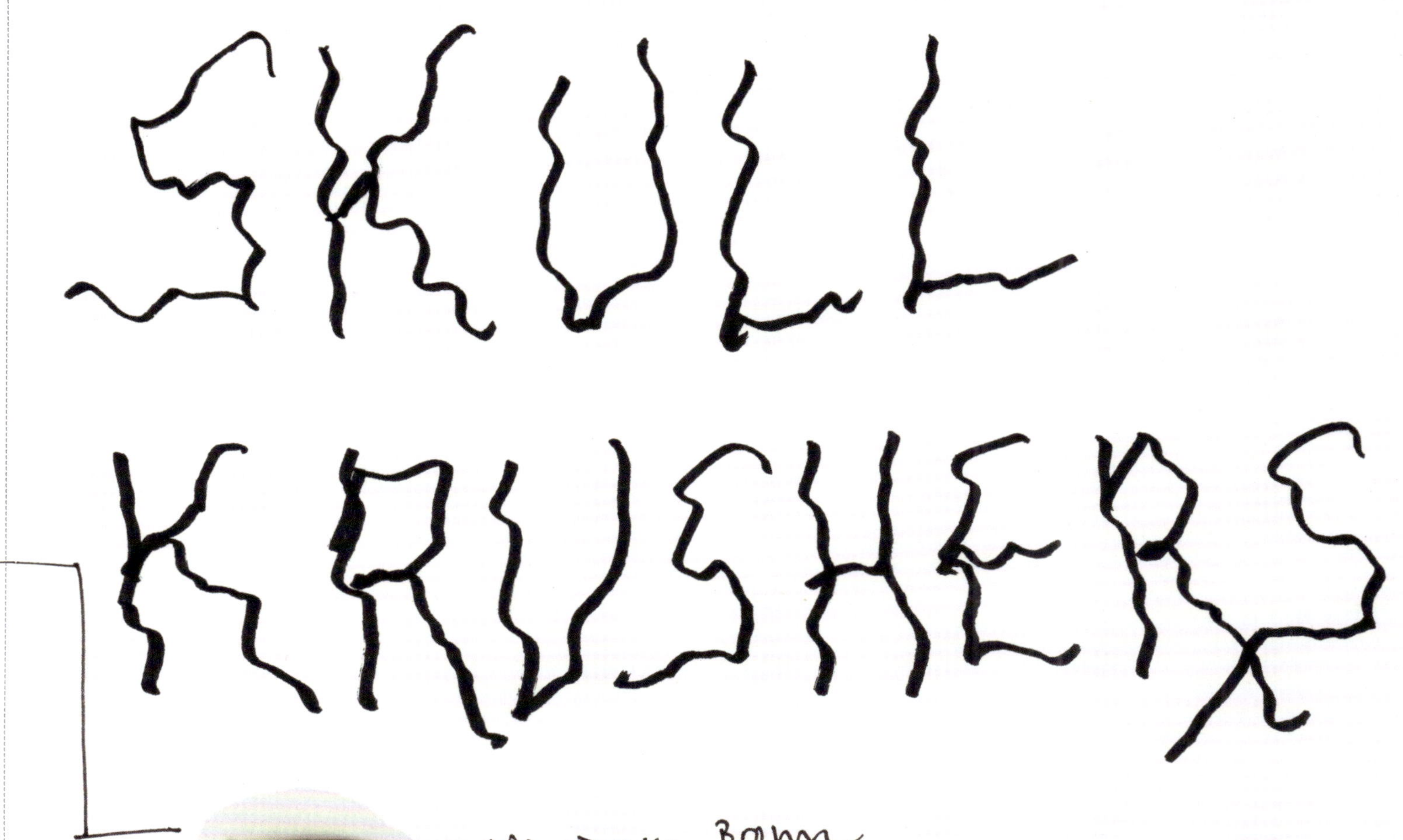

VanDyke Brown
Raw Sienna
Burnt Sienna
Warm White

WarmWhite
OH WarmGrey Light
OH yellow ochre Light

Warmwhite
Titanium white
Radiant Red

Titanium White
Emerald Green
↓ Portland Grey Deep

Pour Homme,
un parfum singulièrement masculin.

Parfums
YVES SAINT LAURENT

mafia

QUESTHAVEN

OCT. 18, 2025

After-shave blue

tit/zinc white
cobalt blue
cad yellow light

Eau de toillette cap side (darker/pinker brick)

Irridescent copper (WB)
Alizarin ~~copper~~ crimson
Raw Umber

Cream in bottle

Flake white
Van Dyke Brown
Naples yellow
Venetian Red

Eau de toilette yellow

Tit/zinc white
~~cad yellow light~~
BISMUTH YELLOW
Naples yellow
Van Dyke Brown
~~Raw Umber~~

~~Alt Perm Red orange~~
~~Pe~~ Cad. Orange

Steel grey blue dark

~~[illegible]~~
paynes grey
~~Cad yellow light~~
Flake White
Van Dyke Brown

Eau de tolet cap top (light/bright brick)

~~dark above +~~
~~zinc white~~
~~Naples yellow~~
~~Cad yellow light~~
~~perm red orange~~

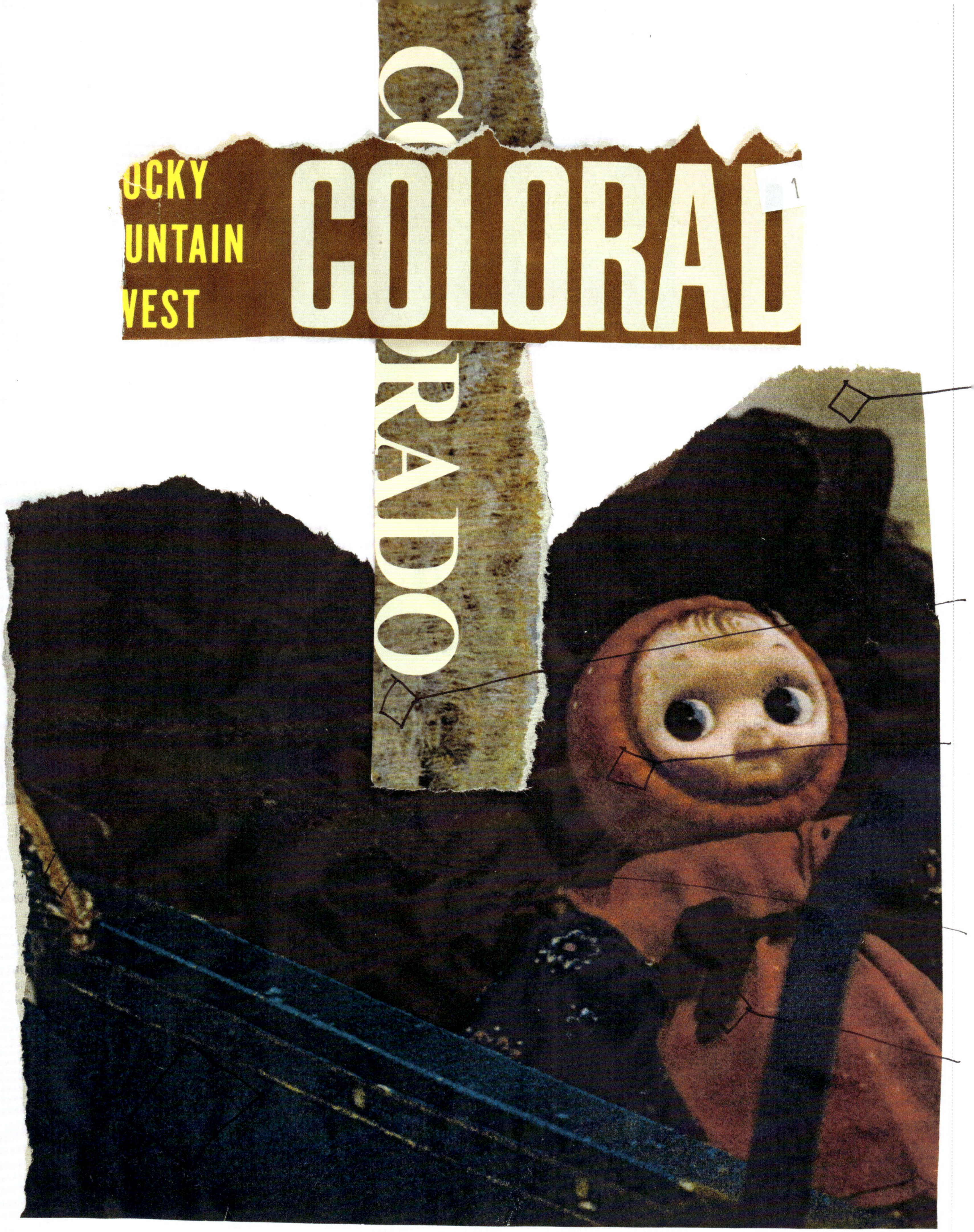

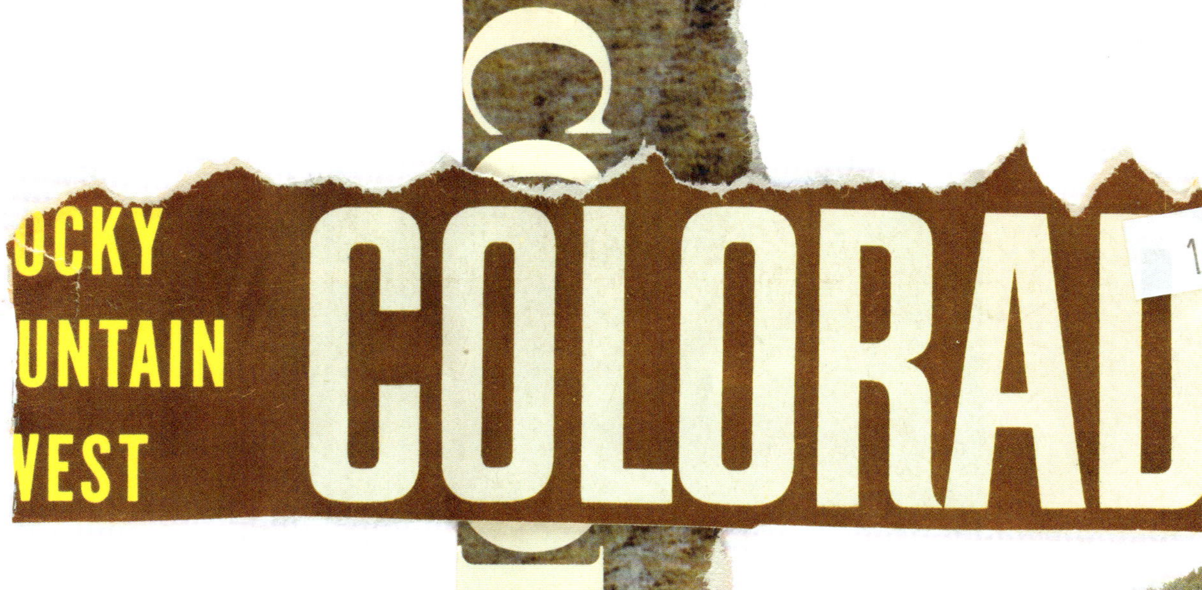
OCKY
UNTAIN
VEST
COLORAD
RADO

Retreat

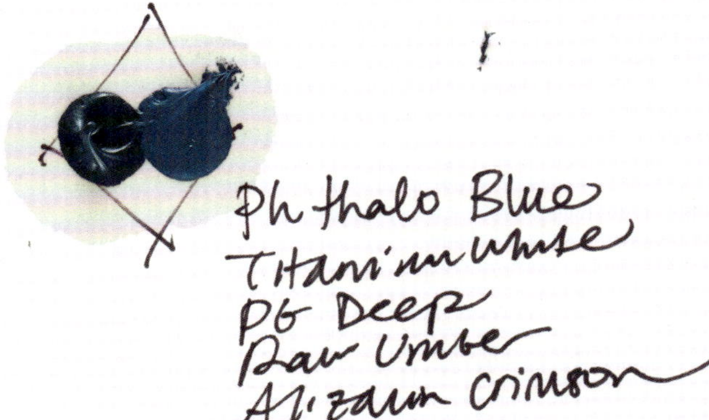

Phthalo Blue
Titanium White
PG Deep
Raw Umber
Alizarin Crimson

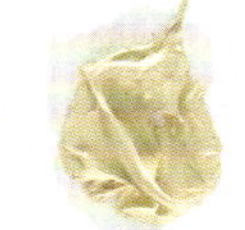

Warm White
Van Dyke Brown
Raw Sienna
Cad Yellow Medium

Titanium White
Portland Grey Medium
Bismuth Vanadate Yellow

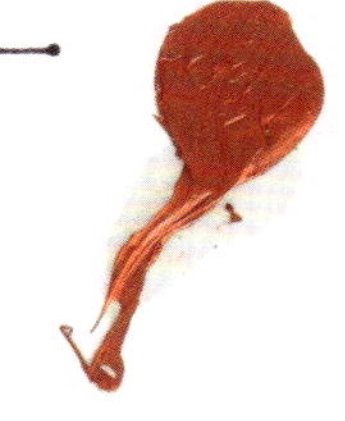

Cadmium Red Medium
Alizarin Crimson
Venetian Red
Cobalt Blue
Warm White
Bismuth Vanadate Yellow

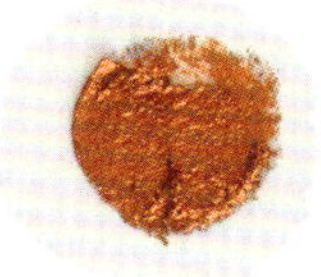

Iridescent Copper

Phthalo Blue
Alizarin Crimson
Van Dyke Brown

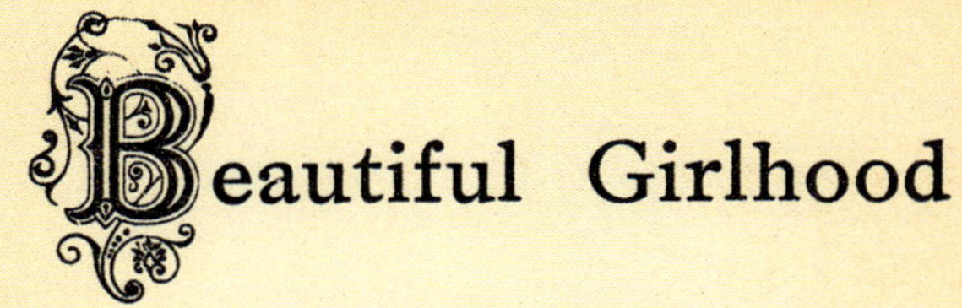

Beautiful Girlhood

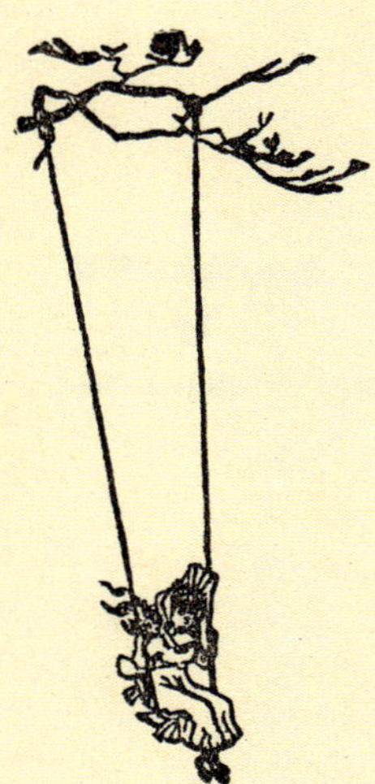

By Mabel Hale

THE WARNER PRESS
Anderson, Indiana

CHAPTER TEN

SINCERITY

"And this I pray, . . . that ye may be sincere and without offence."

TO BE sincere is to be in reality what one appears to be: not feigned; not assumed; genuine, real, and true. How much value we all place upon sincerity! What a low estimate we place upon the friendship of a person who proves not to be sincere, who, when to her advantage, snubs and ignores us. How we despise the actions of one who is lavish with expressions of love and kindness to our face, but who backbites us in our absence. We care nothing for her friendship, and her very expressions of affection are obnoxious. Is it not true that we expect and demand sincerity of our friends?

To be sincere is to be honest; honest with self and honest with others. Honesty costs something. To be truly honest is not always the easiest path. It is an easy matter to deceive ourselves, and to make ourselves believe we are doing right, when down in our hearts we know we are doing wrong. A man might give to a good cause and make himself believe he is doing right, when deep in his heart he must know he gives to gain praise of the people. A girl might make herself think she is studying because she is bent over a book, when she knows her thoughts are all upon the party to which she is going. A boy may make himself think he is smart and manly because he smokes, when deep down in his heart he knows he is being both disobedient and deceitful. There are indeed many ways for us to deceive ourselves. You have heard of the story of King Saul, how he saved alive the best of the sheep and the cattle of the Amalekites, which he had been commanded to utterly destroy. His excuse was that he wanted to make a sacrifice to God of them, when he knew all the time that he saved them to make himself rich. Many a man has built a church or endowed a hospital or school, or performed some other good act, to smother the feelings of regret and the fretting of a wounded conscience.

To be honest with self means to look things over with an unfeigned heart, and to do right because it is right. When we do good that we might appear right in spite of deception in the heart, we deceive ourselves. When we least expect it, our true selves will show out, if we are trying this. Perhaps more people deceive themselves than are ever deceived by others. It pays to be honest with ourselves all the time.

It is just as necessary to be honest with others. Betty buttoned her coat carefully before she left her room, thinking her mother would notice what she had done and approve; for she had often been cautioned against going out in the cold with her coat unbuttoned. But that morning Betty had put on a waist that her mother did not wish her to wear to school, and that was her real reason for carefully buttoning her coat. She was both disobedient and dishonest. We sometimes think that honesty pertains only to money matters. It is true that we should always be honest to the last penny in all business dealings, but honesty also touches every other department of life. To copy or to take advantage in any other way at school in order to gain a grade is just as dishonest in its nature as to steal, or to forge a note. The principle is the same, the difference being only in the magnitude of the deed. To take advantage of the teacher's back being turned to play pranks is also dishonest. To pretend friendship which one does not feel, to smile and approve to the face and laugh to the back, to be two-faced in anything, is mean and dishonest. Honesty, or dishonesty is shown in every little act of life. It is the honest boy or girl who makes the honest citizen. They are the ones whose lives and influence amount to real good in the world's work.

To be sincere is to be hearty; that is, to enter into all we do with all our might. She who is sincere will give the best of herself to whatever work she undertakes. Even the humblest tasks become noble if they are performed heartily. It is a pleasure to watch a girl wash dishes or sweep a floor if she does it with a hearty good-will. As for practising music or studying a lesson, more will be accomplished in half the time if the work is undertaken heartily. The girl who does her work that way is a bit of sunshine in the home. God bless her! She is a comfort and joy every day of her life.

The sincere girl always makes a satisfactory worker wherever she is put. She does her work with a reasonable degree of rapidity and with a will as if she enjoyed it. Whether she works in an office, in the schoolroom, in the factory, or in the kitchen, whether her work brings her good pay or whether she is a busy home-toiler who gets only her board and clothes, if she is sincere and willing she will be a success. Her eye is not on the clock to see if her time is about up, but her whole attention is upon what she is doing. Sincere people are hearty in their friendships. Did you ever put your hand into the hand of a friend and have her grasp it with a hearty good-will and look you in the face with a friendly greeting? Did it not do you good? It does others just as much good if you greet them heartily. Again, I have offered my hand to women who gave me the tips of their fingers in a delicate, afraid-of-you manner that chilled all my ardor. I did not like it, and others will not like it if you meet them that way. The handshake is quite an index to people's hearts. Those who are hearty and sincere are not afraid to let you know it.

To be sincere is to be unfeigned—no pretension, no putting on. The girl who is sincere means every word she says when she is expressing love and friendship. I need not fear that she is only trying to make an impression on me, nor that she is getting my confidence only to ridicule me later. She is no turncoat and no traitor. It seems to me a girl can have no greater fault than feigning friendship and affection she does not feel. Those who are sincere are real. They are real friends, real students, real sisters, real Christians.

To be sincere is to be frank. Frankness helps a girl to speak right out from the heart what she thinks and feels. But there is a very unpleasant trait that sometimes passes as frankness. That is a disposition to say cutting things. There are many things that are better left unsaid. Even though circumstances have given ample room for severe criticism, it is better to keep the bitter word unsaid, and to speak kindly. Frankness does not mean that we shall tell people what we think of them and their doings on all occasions. True frankness shows in clear, honest eyes and in a gaze of purity and truth, which brings confidence to all who see it. It will speak out of the eyes when the lips are silent. She who is frank keeps nothing back that changes the meaning of what she says.

Beautiful girlhood can hold no more attractive nor lovable trait than sincerity. When a girl can look with honest eyes and perfect sincerity into life, and can meet the temptations that are sure to come with a

heart sincerely set to do God's will, that girl will succeed. Her life will be a blessing to many. Old and young will be encouraged and strengthened by her presence and friendship.

SNOUTITUDE 2025

oil on canvas
33 × 28"

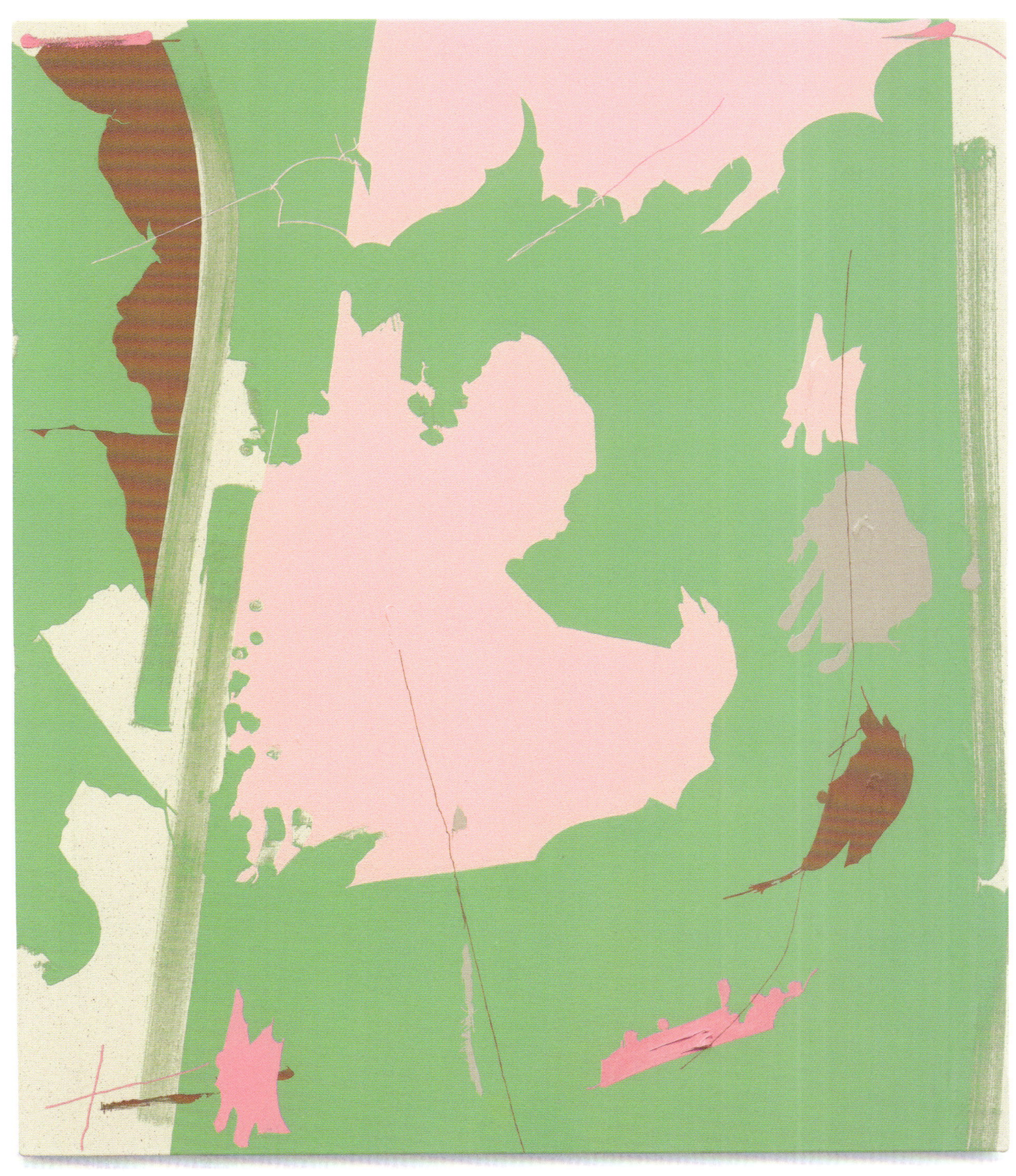

MAYSHA THE FOOL 2025

oil on canvas
33 × 28"

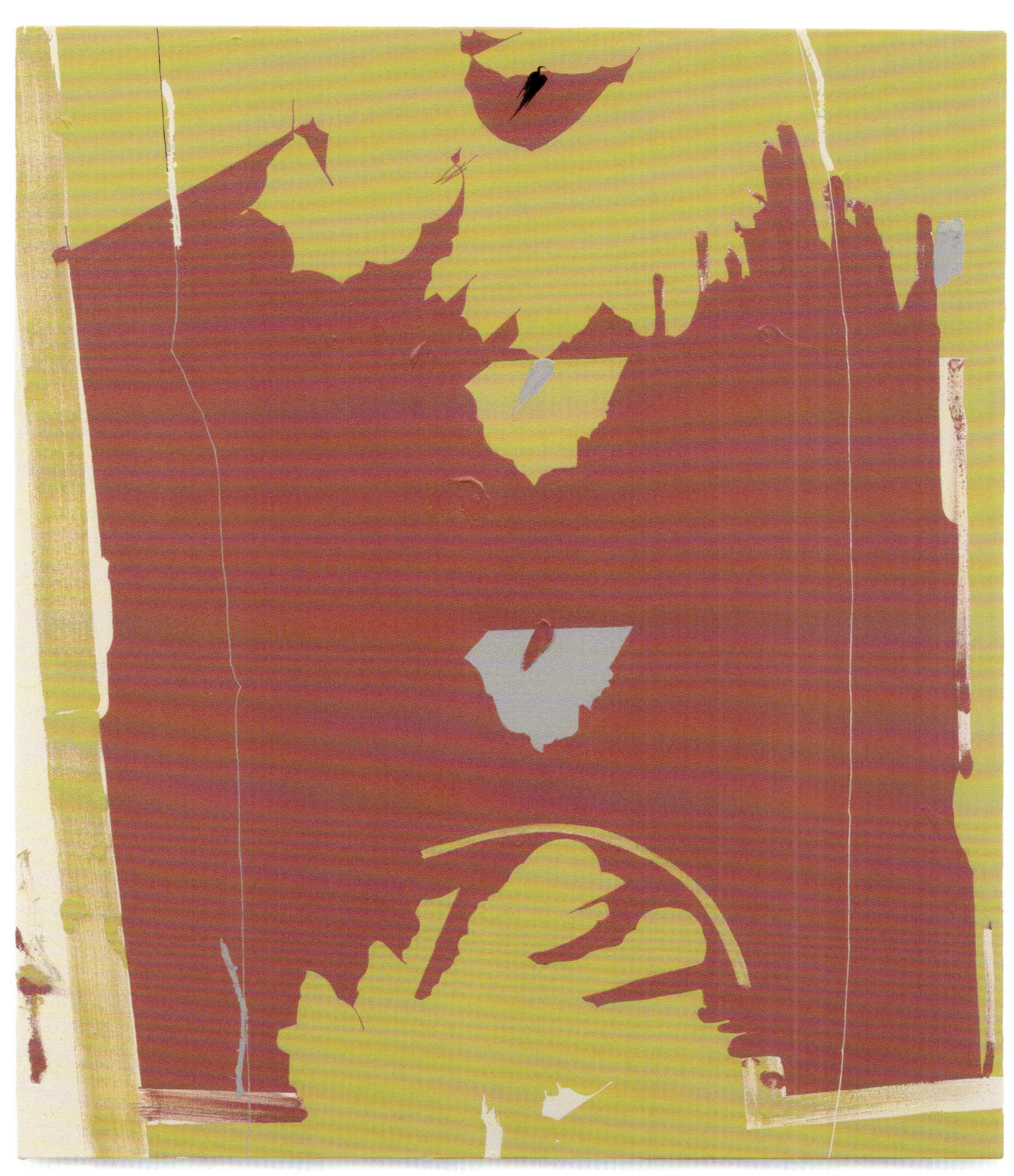

HAPPY NOWRUZ 2025

oil on canvas
15 × 17"

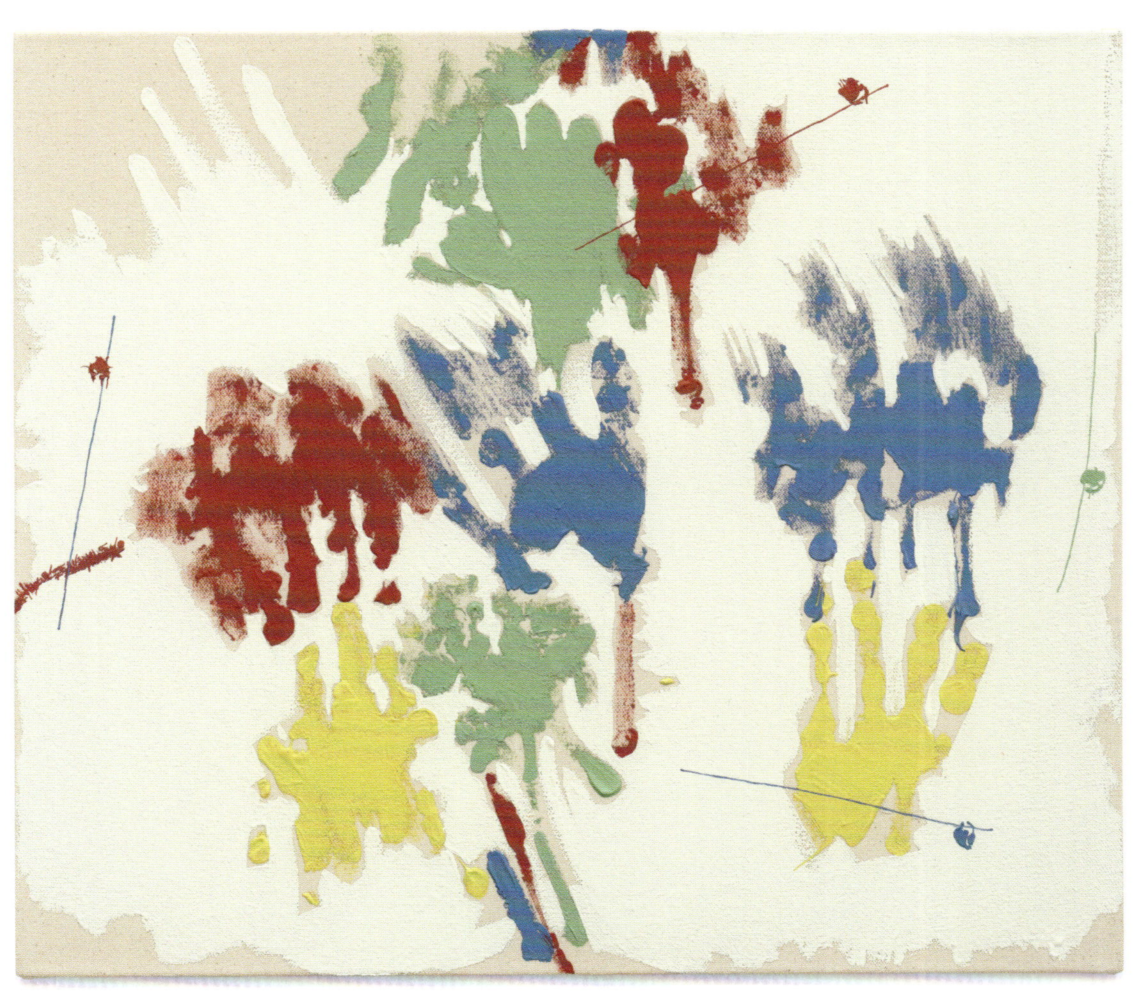

ABSOLUTE ZERO 2025

oil on canvas
49 × 41"

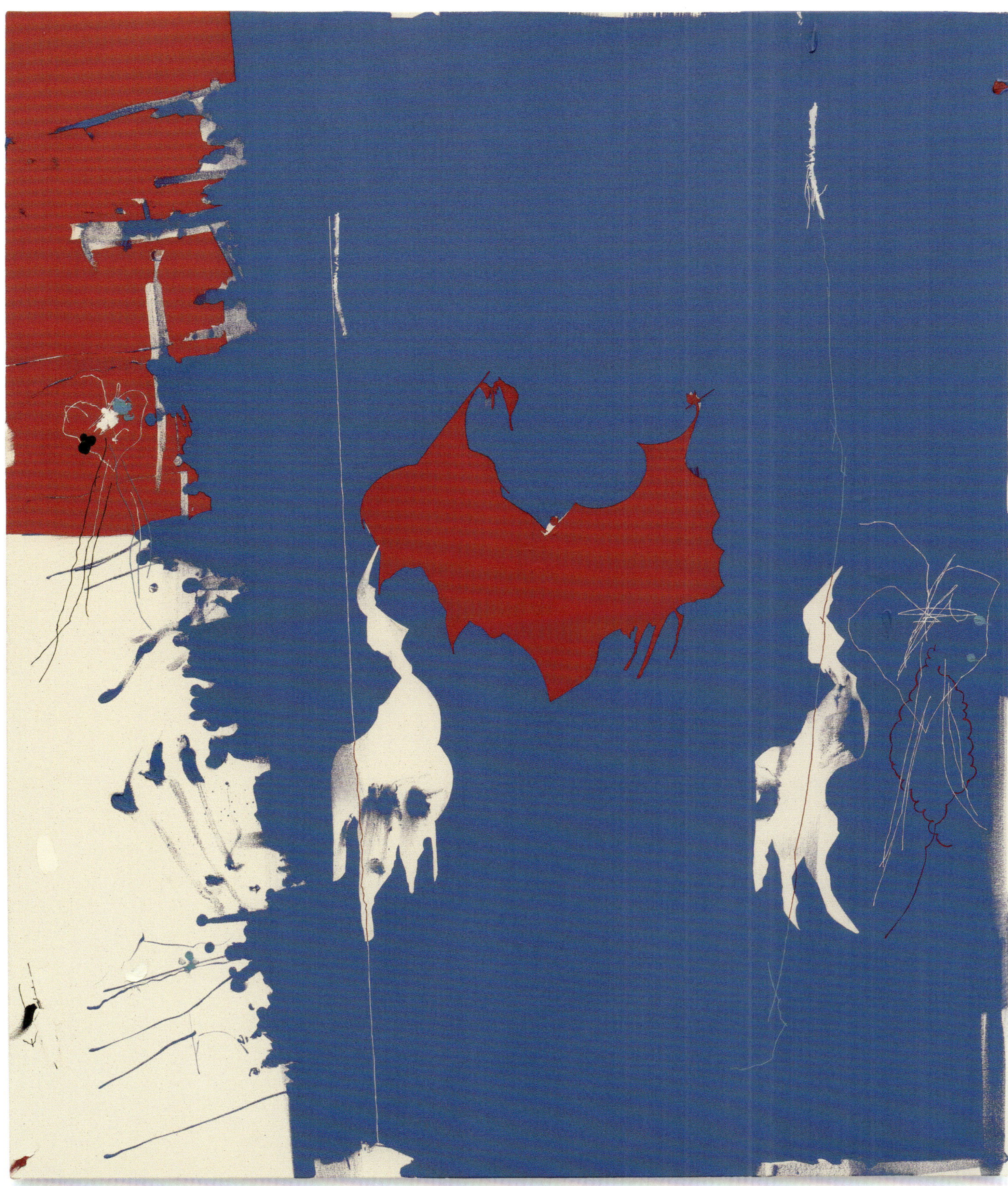

SADDOZAY 2025

oil on canvas
49 × 41"

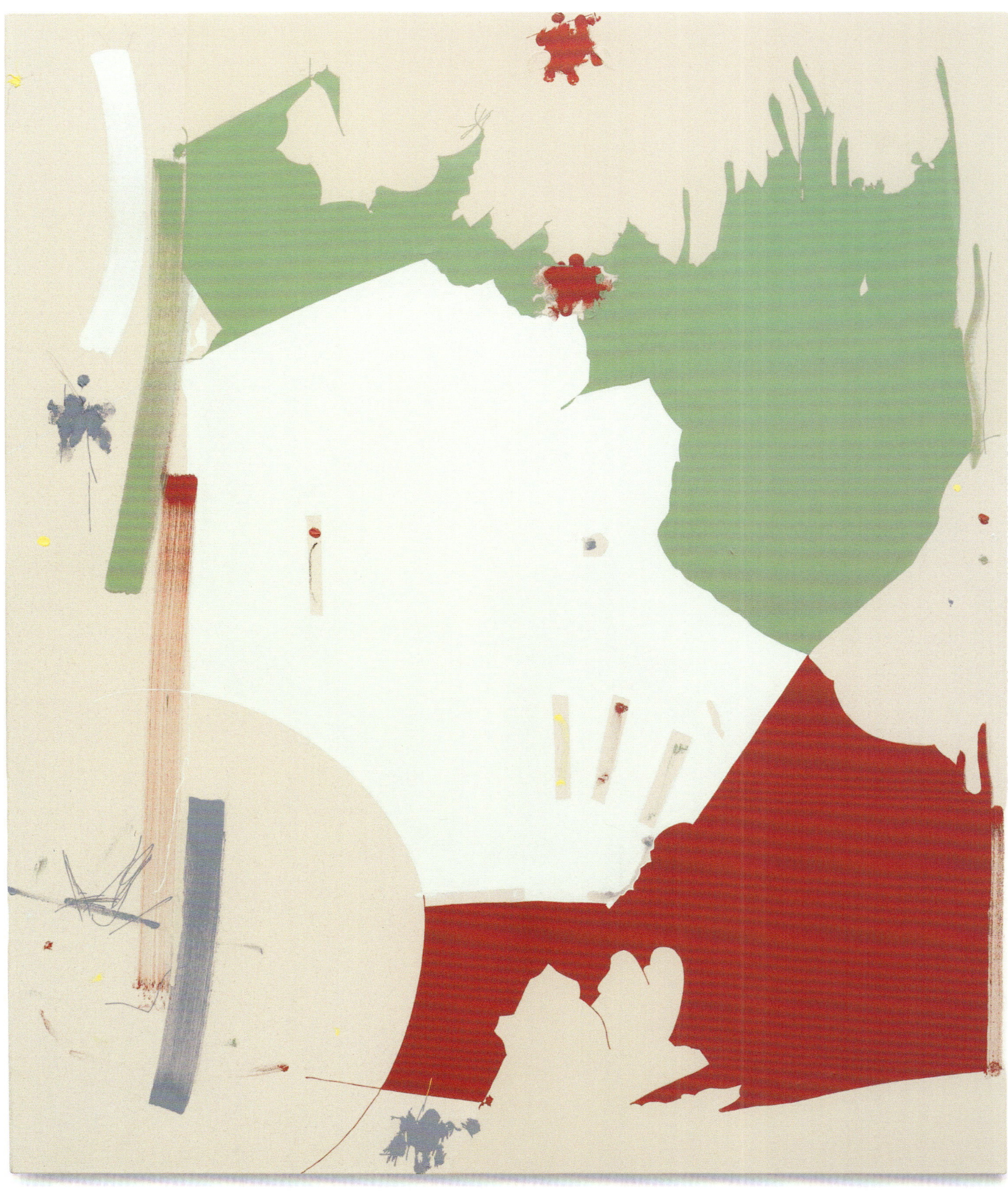

DEAD LIFT 2025

oil on canvas
49 × 41"

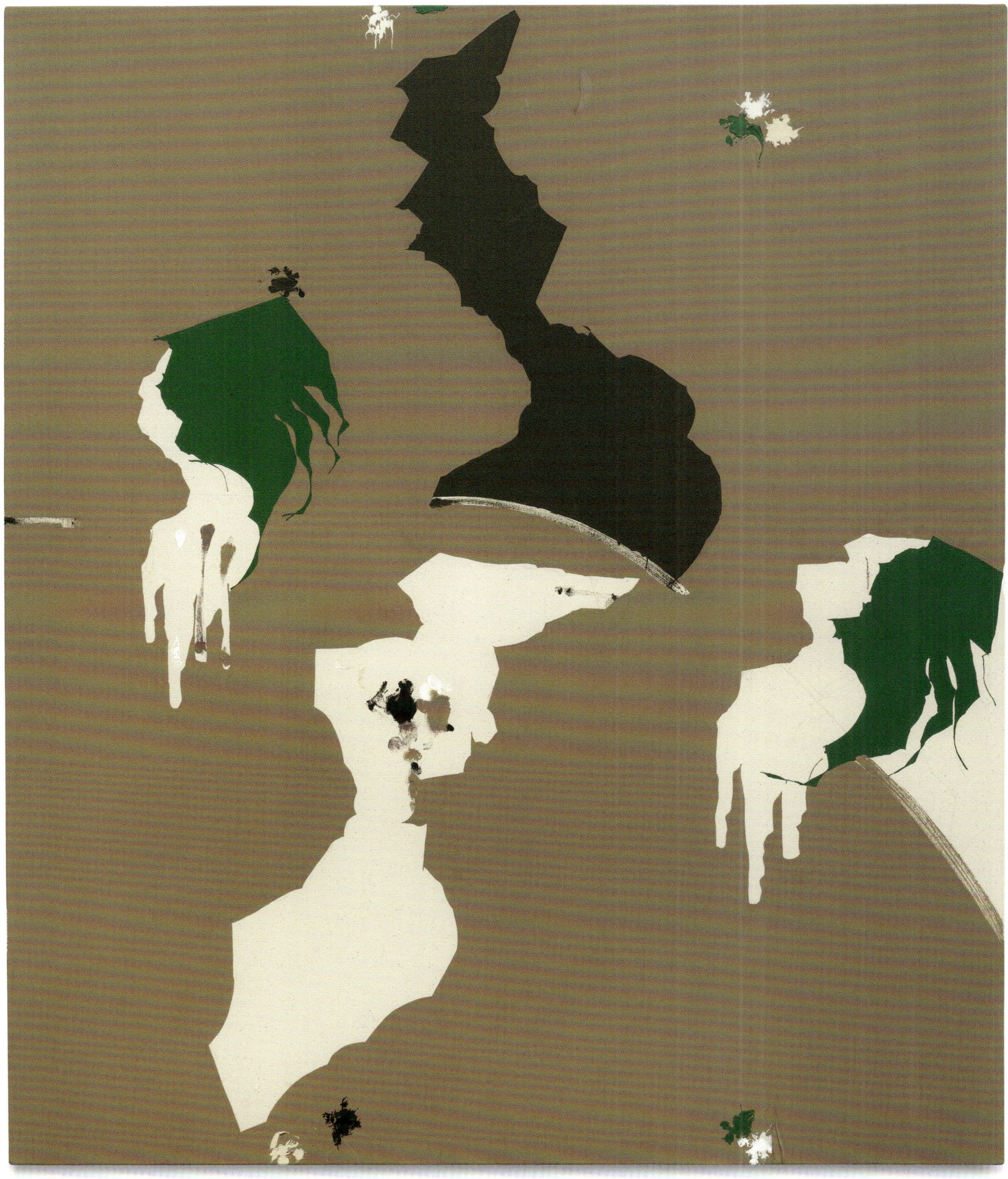

SKY LEILA 2025

oil on canvas
33 × 28"

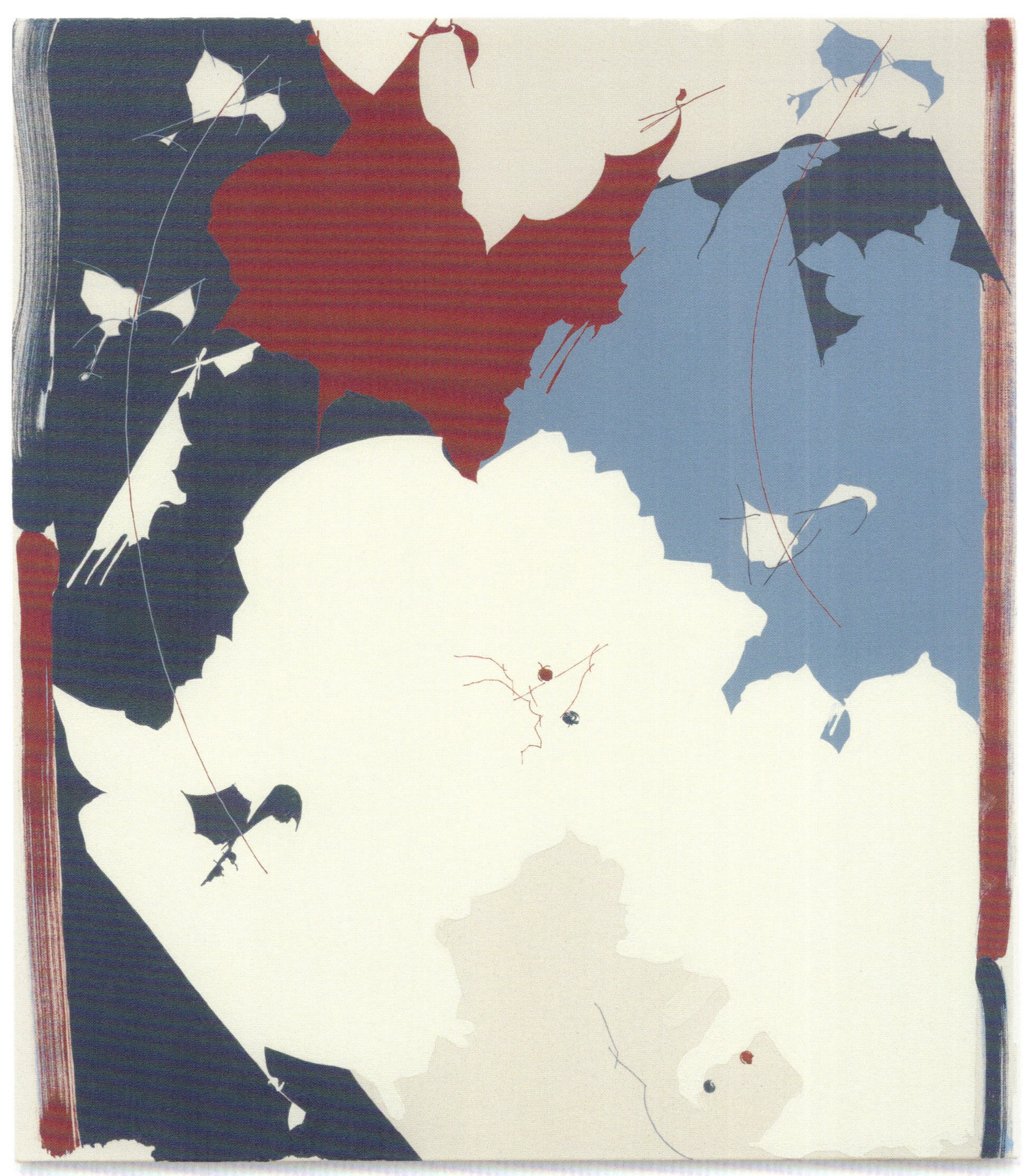

I DON'T MIND WHAT HAPPENS 2025

oil on canvas
15 × 17"

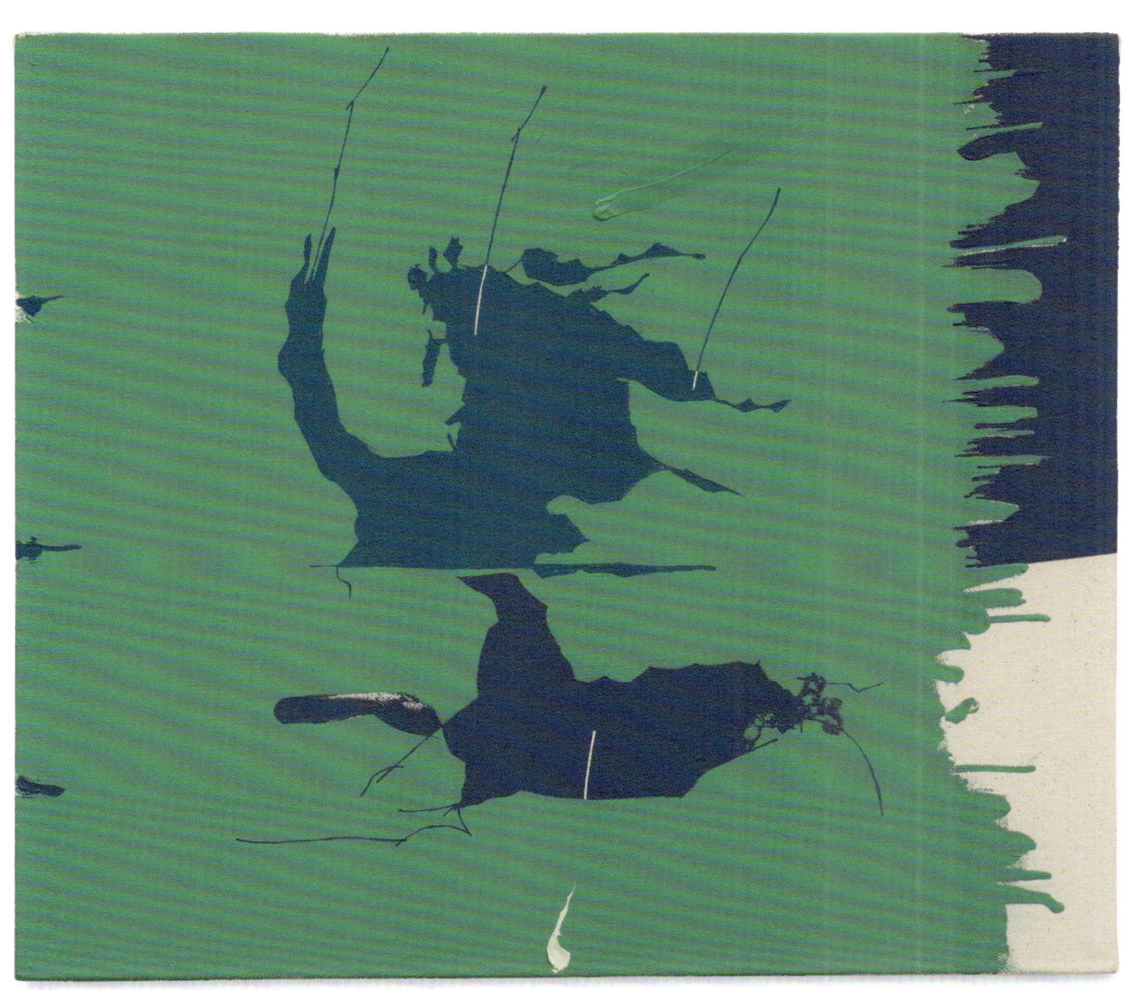

WIT 2025

oil on canvas
17 × 15"

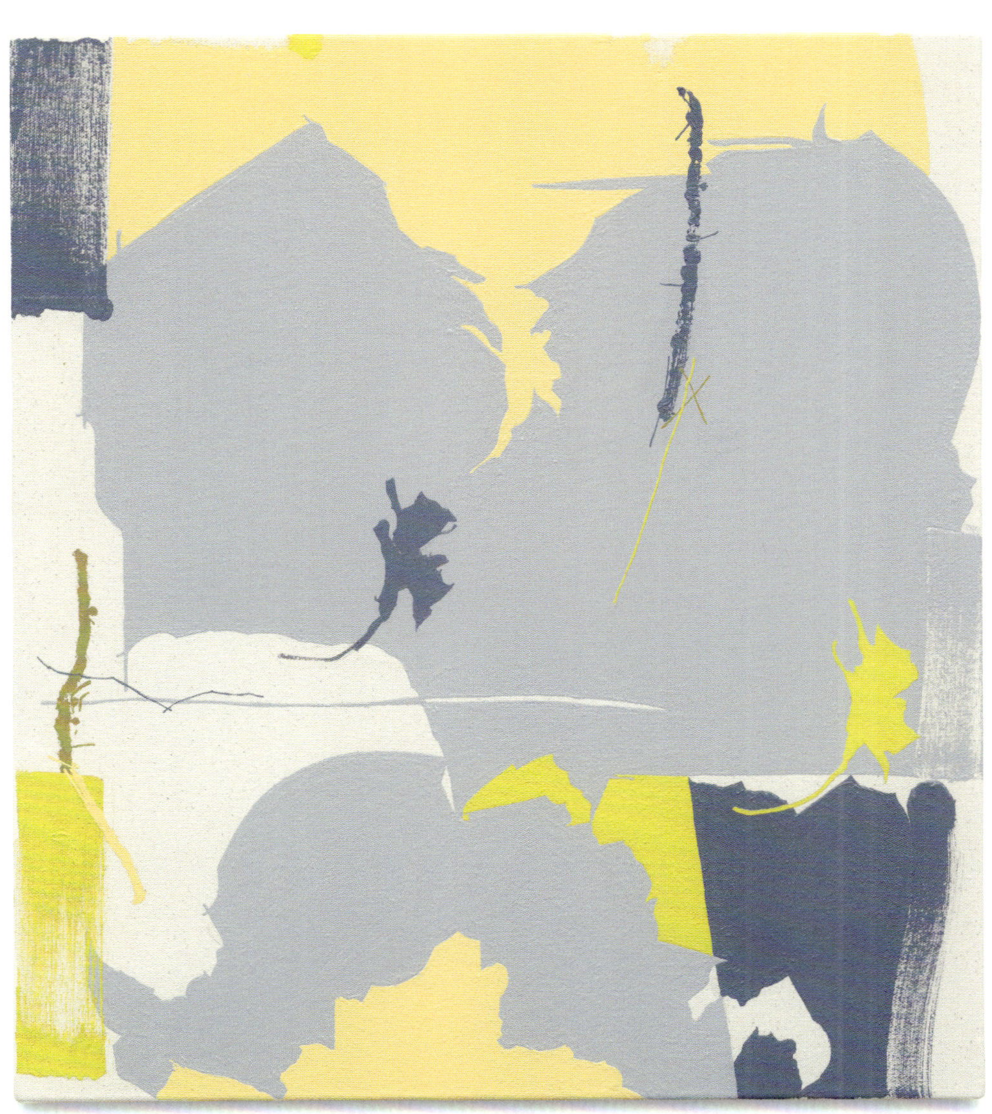

O THY LIVING GOD; UNLOCK THESE HANDS; UNLOCK THIS HEART; AMEN 2025

oil on canvas
93 × 106"

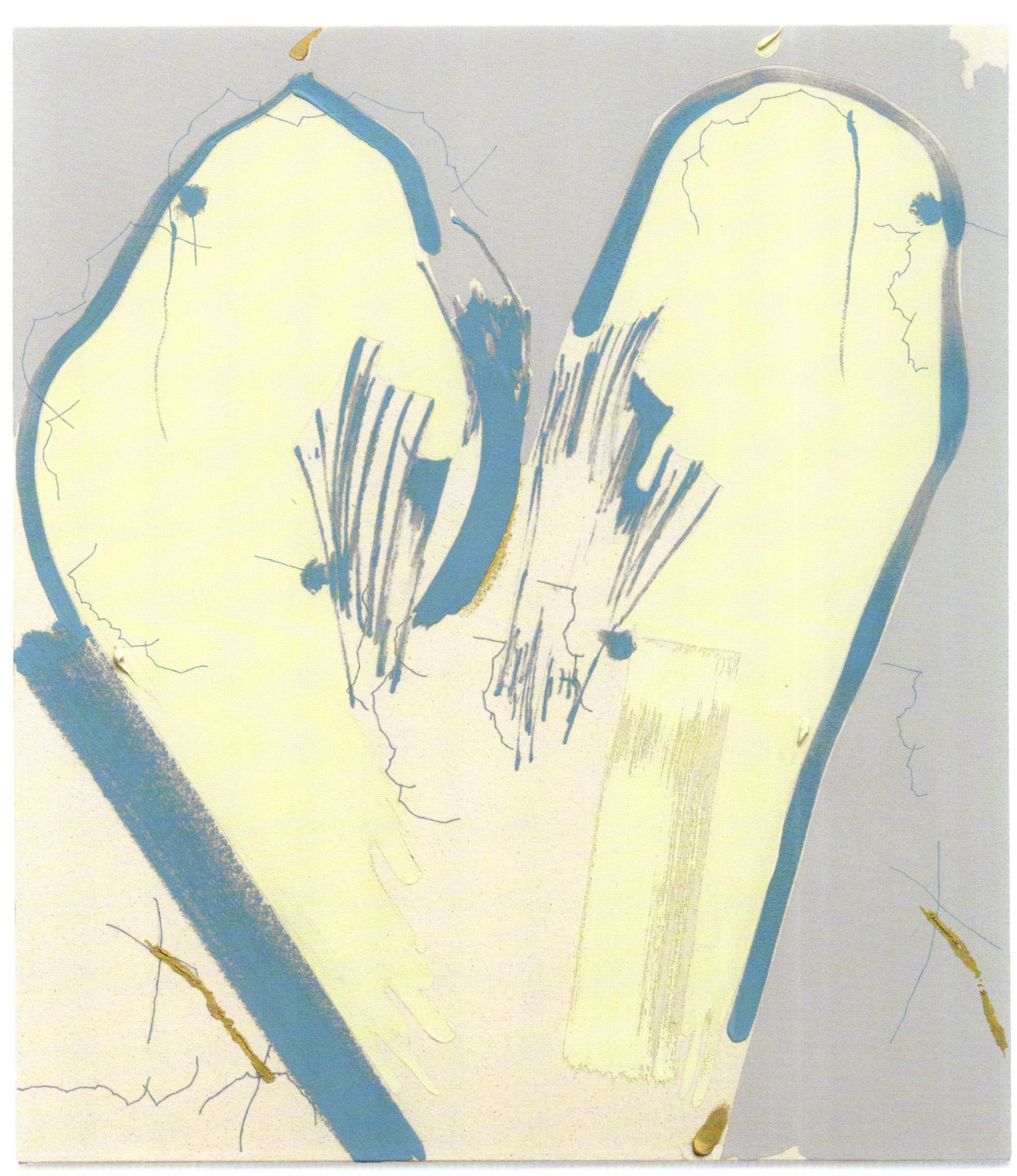

AUDITION 2025

oil on canvas
17 × 15"

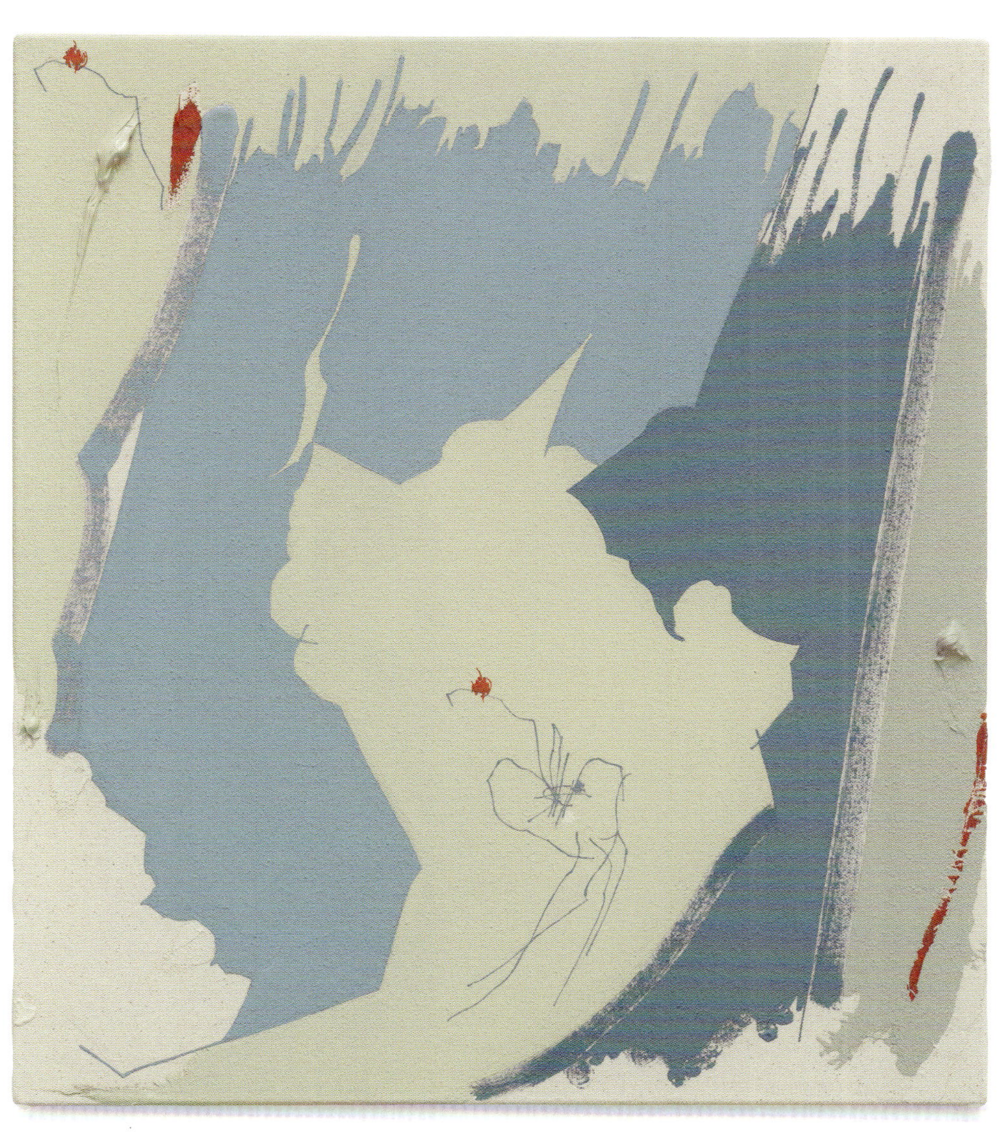

SKULL KRUSHERS 2025

oil on canvas
33 × 28"

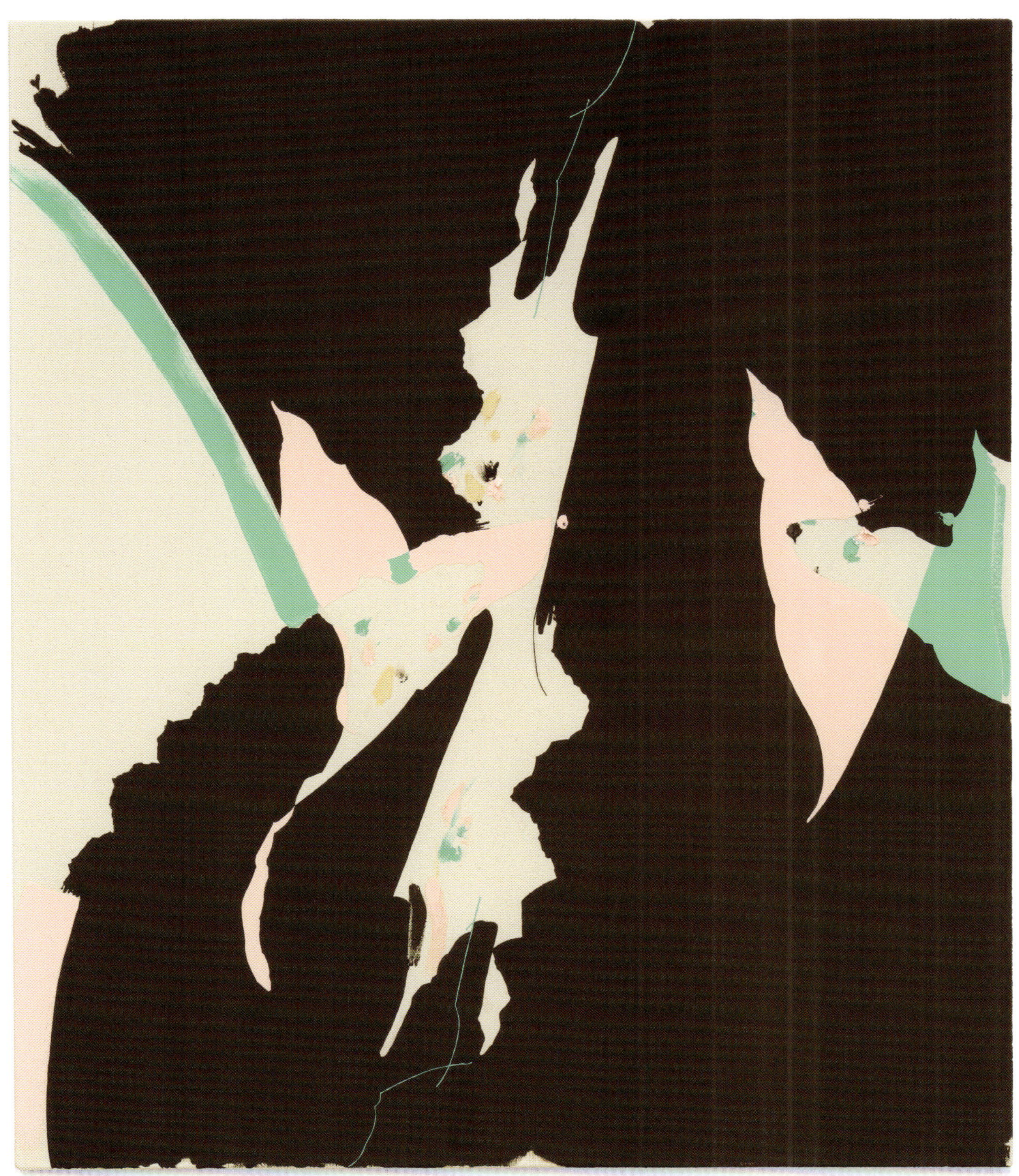

QUESTHAVEN 2025

oil on canvas
33 × 28"

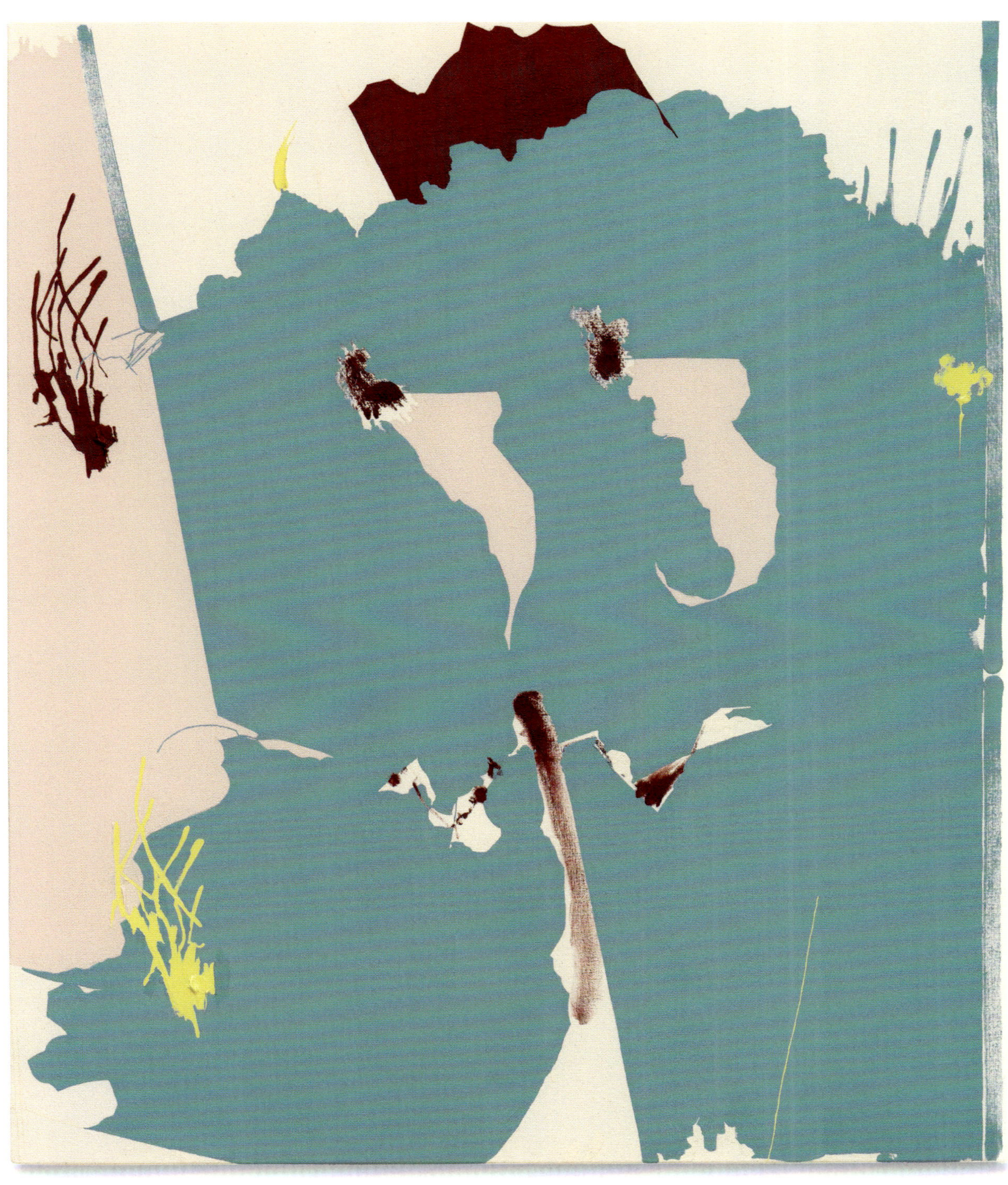

RETREAT 2025

oil on canvas
17 × 15"

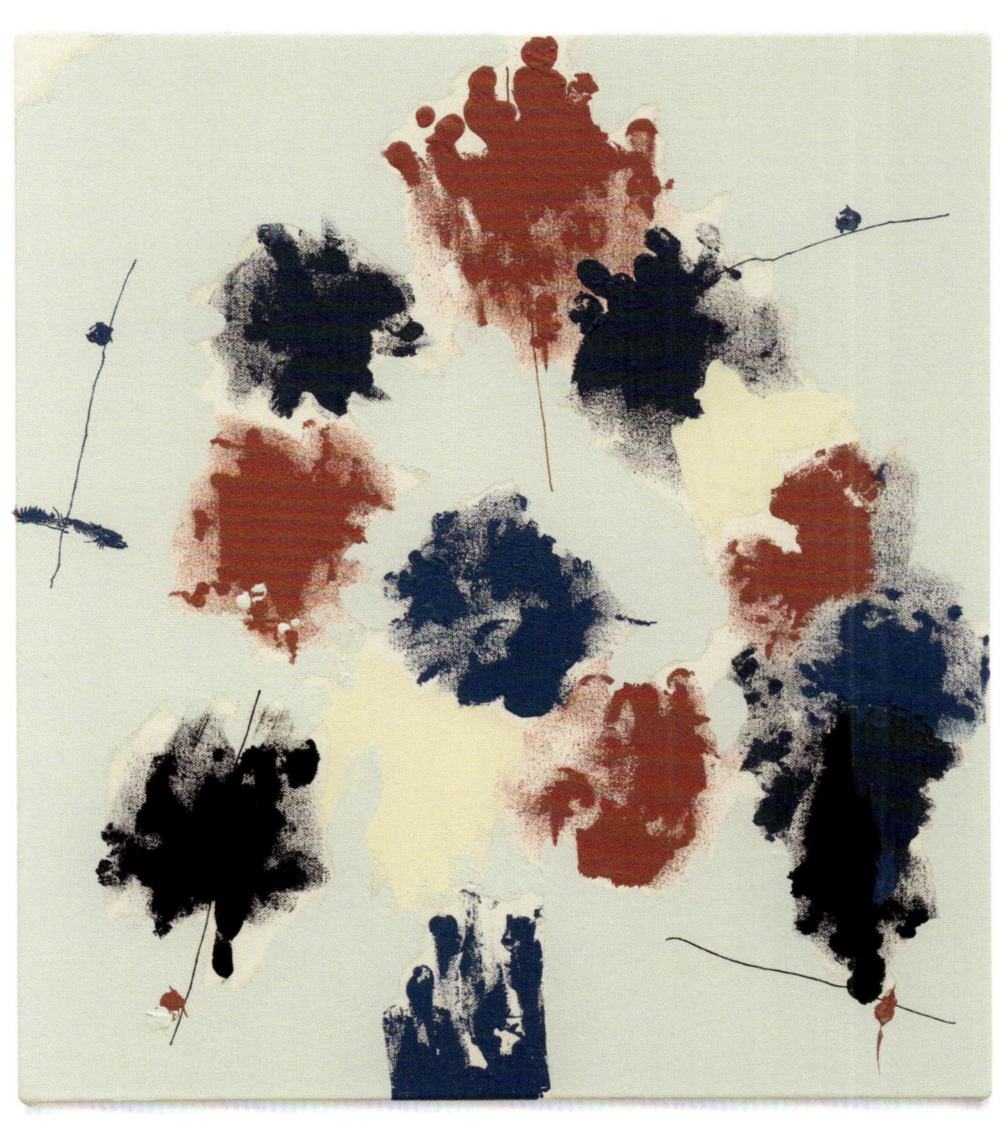

LIST OF WORKS

44 **SNOUTITUDE 2025**
oil on canvas
33 × 28"

46 **MAYSHA THE FOOL 2025**
oil on canvas
33 × 28"

48 **HAPPY NOWRUZ 2025**
oil on canvas
15 × 17"

50 **ABSOLUTE ZERO 2025**
oil on canvas
49 × 41"

52 **SADDOZAY 2025**
oil on canvas
49 × 41"

54 **DEAD LIFT 2025**
oil on canvas
49 × 41"

56 **SKY LEILA 2025**
oil on canvas
33 × 28"

58 **I DON'T MIND WHAT HAPPENS 2025**
oil on canvas
15 × 17"

60 **WIT 2025**
oil on canvas
17 × 15"

62 **O THY LIVING GOD; UNLOCK THESE HANDS; UNLOCK THIS HEART; AMEN 2025**
oil on canvas
93 × 106"

64 **ANGEL 2025**
oil on canvas
33 × 28"

66 **AUDITION 2025**
oil on canvas
17 × 15"

68 **SKULL KRUSHERS 2025**
oil on canvas
33 × 28"

70 **QUESTHAVEN 2025**
oil on canvas
33 × 28"

72 **RETREAT 2025**
oil on canvas
17 × 15"

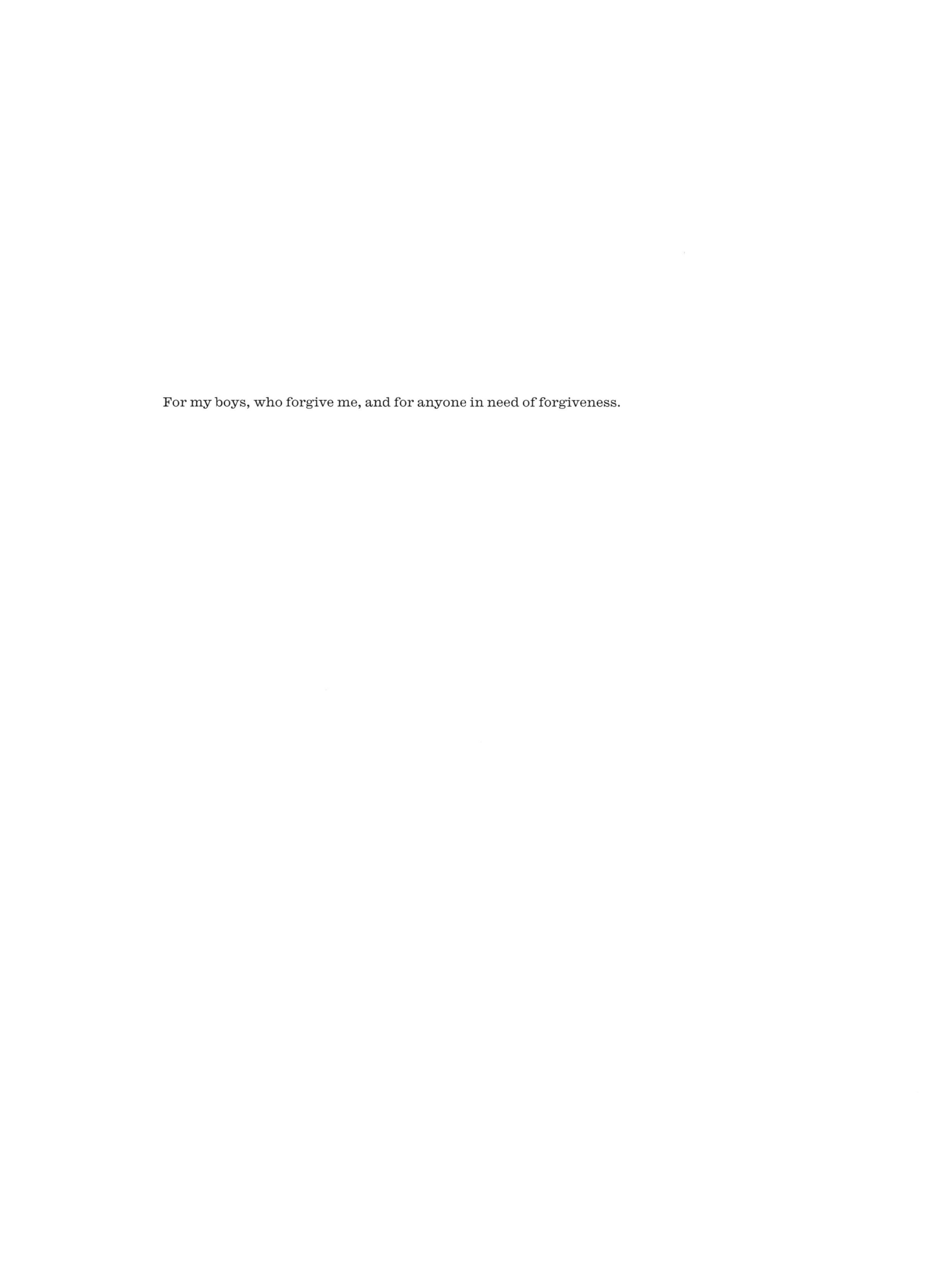

For my boys, who forgive me, and for anyone in need of forgiveness.

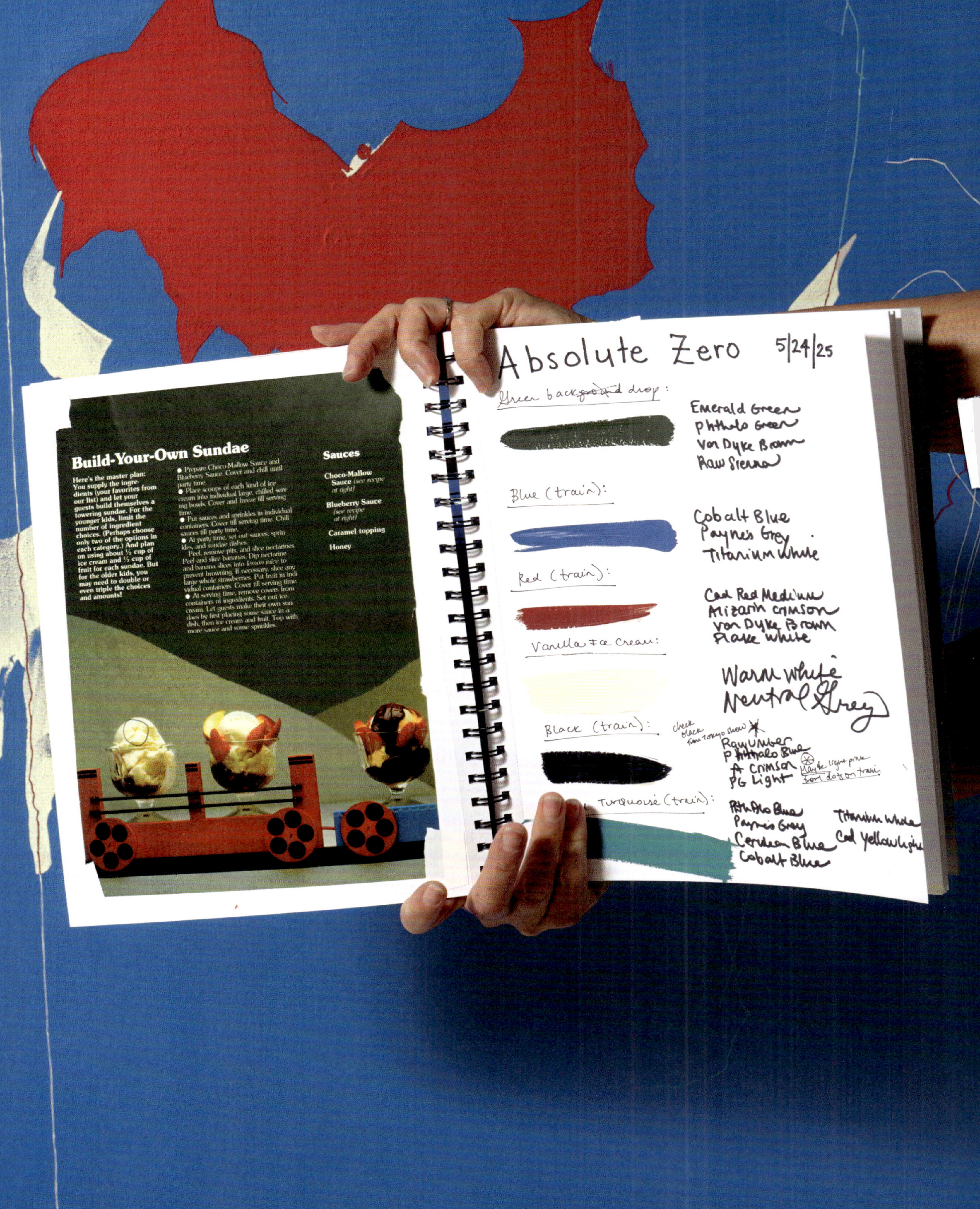
Build-Your-Own Sundae
Here's the master plan: You supply the ingredients (your favorites from our list) and let your guests build themselves a towering sundae. For the younger kids, limit the number of ingredient choices. (Perhaps choose only two of the options in each category.) And plan on using about ½ cup of ice cream and ⅓ cup of fruit for each sundae. But for the older kids, you may need to double or even triple the choices and amounts!
● Prepare Choco-Mallow Sauce and Blueberry Sauce. Cover and chill until party time.
● Place scoops of each kind of ice cream into individual large, chilled serv ing bowls. Cover and freeze till serving time.
● Put sauces and sprinkles in individual containers. Cover till serving time. Chill sauces till party time.
● At party time, set out sauces, sprin kles, and sundae dishes.
Peel, remove pits, and slice nectarines. Peel and slice bananas. Dip nectarine and banana slices into lemon juice to prevent browning. If necessary, slice any large whole strawberries. Put fruit in indi vidual containers. Cover till serving time.
● At serving time, remove covers from containers of ingredients. Set out ice cream. Let guests make their own sun daes by first placing some sauce in a dish, then ice cream and fruit. Top with more sauce and some sprinkles.
Sauces
Choco-Mallow Sauce (see recipe at right)
Blueberry Sauce (see recipe at right)
Caramel topping
Honey
Absolute Zero
5/24/25
Green backdrop:
Emerald Green
Phthalo Green
Van Dyke Brown
Raw Sienna
Blue (train):
Cobalt Blue
Payne's Grey
Titanium White
Red (train):
Cad Red Medium
Alizarin Crimson
Van Dyke Brown
Flake White
Vanilla Ice Cream:
Warm White
Neutral Grey
Black (train):
check black from Tokyo show
Raw Umber
Phthalo Blue
A Crimson
PG Light
Maybe light pink from dots on train
Turquoise (train):
Phthalo Blue
Payne's Grey
Cerulean Blue
Cobalt Blue
Titanium White
Cad Yellow light

Published on the occasion of
Maysha Mohamedi
Maysha the Fool
March 10 – April 25, 2026

Pace Gallery
540 West 25th Street
New York

Publication © 2026 Pace Publishing
Artworks by Maysha Mohamedi © Maysha Mohamedi

"Sincerity" by Mabel Hale reprinted from *Beautiful Girlhood*
(The Warner Press, 1922), 70–76.

All rights reserved. No part of this publication may be reproduced or transmitted in any form or by any means, electronic or mechanical, including photocopying, recording, or any information storage and retrieval system, without permission in writing from the publisher.

Every reasonable effort has been made to identify owners of copyright. Errors or omissions will be corrected in subsequent editions.

Photography:
Christopher DeWitt II: cover
Jeff McLane: pp. 1–79

Creative Director: Tomo Makiura
Design: Tara Stewart
Production: Paul Pollard
Editor in Chief: Gillian Canavan
Editorial Manager: Madeline Gilmore
Rights & Reproductions: Vincent Wilcke
Color Separations: Altaimage, New York
Printing: Meridian Printing, a GHP Media company

Typeset in Caslon Ionic

ISBN: 978-1-948701-85-3
Library of Congress Control Number: 2026931291

Available through ARTBOOK | D.A.P.
75 Broad Street, Suite 630 New York, NY 10004
www.artbook.com